CW00501607

OPERATION COMPASS

OPERATION COMPASS

TEXT BY
JON LATIMER

BATTLESCENE PLATES
JIM LAURIER

OSPREY
HISTORY

First published in Great Britain in 2000 by Osprey Publishing, Elms Court, Chapel Way, Botley, Oxford OX2 9LP, United Kingdom
Email: info@ospreypublishing.com

© 2000 Osprey Publishing Ltd.

Also published as Campaign 73: *Operation Compass 1940*

ISBN 1 84176 280 6

Editor: Marcus Cowper
Design: The Black Spot
Index by Alan Rutter
Origination by Grasmere Digital Imaging, Leeds, UK
Colour bird's eye view illustrations by The Black Spot
Cartography by The Map Studio
Battlescene artwork by Jim Laurier
Printed in China through World Print Ltd.

01 02 03 04 05 10 9 8 7 6 5 4 3 2 1

FOR A CATALOGUE OF ALL BOOKS PUBLISHED BY OSPREY MILITARY AND AVIATION PLEASE WRITE TO:

The Marketing Manager, Osprey Direct UK,
PO Box 140, Wellingborough, Northants,
NN8 4ZA, United Kingdom.
Email: info@ospreydirect.co.uk

The Marketing Manager, Osprey Direct USA,
c/o Motorbooks International, PO Box 1, Osceola,
WI 54020-0001, USA.
Email: info@ospreydirectusa.com

www.ospreypublishing.com

Artist's Note

Readers may care to note that the original paintings from which the colour plates in this book were prepared are available for private sale. All reproduction copyright whatsoever is retained by the publisher. All enquiries should be addressed to:

Jim Laurier, PO Box 1118, Keene, NH 03431, USA
http://aviation-art.simplenet.com

The publishers regret that they can enter into no correspondence on this matter.

KEY TO MILITARY SYMBOLS

FRONT COVER: **A mass of Matilda tanks on the move. (Tank Museum - 1767/B3)**

BACK COVER: **British transport passing a burning Italian tank in the open desert. (Tank Museum - 3576/E2)**

PAGE 2 **The Cruiser Tanks Mark IV and VIA (A13) had 1$\frac{1}{4}$in. (30mm) of armour and a top speed of 30mph (48km/h) and outclassed the Italian M13. The design was based on the American Christie suspension. Like other British tanks of the period however, it was only armed with a 2-pdr. gun and co-axial machine-gun (.303in. Vickers in the Mk IV, $\frac{1}{3}$in. (7.92mm) Besa in the Mk IVA). 335 were eventually built. (Tank Museum – 2555/E3)**

CONTENTS

ORIGINS OF THE CAMPAIGN 7

OPPOSING COMMANDERS 14

Italian Commanders • British Commanders

OPPOSING FORCES 17

Italian Forces • British and Commonwealth Forces

OPPOSING PLANS 27

THE CAMPAIGN 32

The Five Day Raid • Bardia • Tobruk • Derna • Beda Fomm

AFTERMATH 86

CHRONOLOGY 89

BIBLIOGRAPHY 90

WARGAMING THE CAMPAIGN 93

INDEX 96

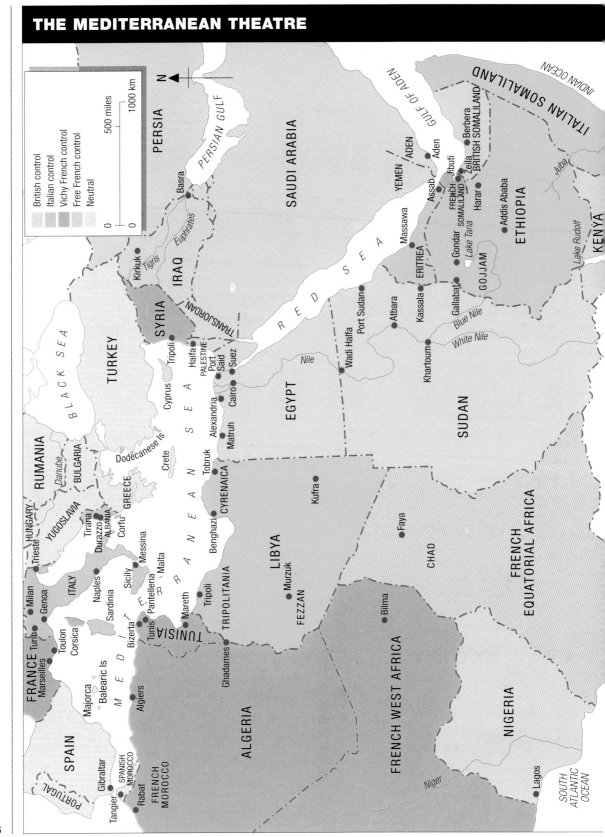

Legend:
- British control
- Italian control
- Vichy French control
- Free French control
- Neutral

Scale: 500 miles / 1000 km

N

PERSIA
PERSIAN GULF
SAUDI ARABIA
GULF OF ADEN
INDIAN OCEAN
ITALIAN SOMALILAND
Berbera
BRITISH SOMALILAND
Zella
ADEN
Aden
Jibuti
Assab
FRENCH SOMALILAND
Harar
Addis Ababa
ETHIOPIA
Juba
Basra
YEMEN
Massawa
ERITREA
Gondar
Lake Tana
GOJJAM
KENYA
Lake Rudolf
Kirkuk
Tigris
Euphrates
IRAQ
SYRIA
TRANSJORDAN
Port Sudan
Atbara
Kassala
Gallabat
Blue Nile
White Nile
Khartoum
Tripoli
Haifa
PALESTINE
Port Said
Suez
Nile
Wadi Halfa
BLACK SEA
TURKEY
Cyprus
Alexandria
Matruh
Cairo
EGYPT
SUDAN
RUMANIA
Danube
HUNGARY
BULGARIA
YUGOSLAVIA
GREECE
Dodecanese Is
Crete
Tobruk
CYRENAICA
Benghazi
Kufra
Trieste
Tirana
Durazzo
ALBANIA
Corfu
Messina
Sicily
Malta
LIBYA
Murzuk
FEZZAN
Faya
CHAD
FRENCH EQUATORIAL AFRICA
Turin
Milan
Genoa
ITALY
Naples
Sardinia
Pantelleria
Mareth
Tripoli
TRIPOLITANIA
FRANCE
Marseilles
Toulon
Corsica
Bizerta
Tunis
TUNISIA
Ghadames
Bilma
FRENCH WEST AFRICA
NIGERIA
Majorca
Balearic Is
Algiers
ALGERIA
Niger
Lagos
SPAIN
Gibraltar
SPANISH MOROCCO
Tangier
Rabat
FRENCH MOROCCO
PORTUGAL
SOUTH ATLANTIC OCEAN
MEDITERRANEAN SEA
RED SEA

OPERATION COMPASS

ORIGINS OF THE CAMPAIGN

With France on the verge of collapse and Britain routed from the continent, the Italian Fascist dictator, Benito Mussolini, declared war on both countries on 10 June 1940. He remarked cynically that he 'needed a few thousand dead so that he could sit at the conference table as one who has fought'. He got them. Tough French alpine troops administered a sound thrashing to the Italians before the armistice was signed two weeks later. Mussolini's advisors had warned him that the Italian armed forces were neither adequately trained nor equipped to undertake a modern European war; but then, he did not expect to. With France defeated it seemed only a matter of months before Britain too would be brought to her knees. Italy's armies vastly outnumbered the British and the revitalised Italian fleet of the *Regia Marina* (Italian Navy) also outnumbered the Royal Navy. Despite the latter's aircraft carrier capability, it seemed the aircraft of the land-based *Regia Aeronautica* (Italian Air Force) would further enhance their superiority.

In the early summer of 1940, the Mediterranean had appeared relatively quiet. Now it changed suddenly. Hitler heard over dinner on 11 June that the Italians had bombed Malta. He was dismissive of the action, believing that if Mussolini was serious he would be invading the tiny island. Indeed, he little knew then how much grief it would cause him when, having finally sent assistance to his Latin ally, he would suffer enormous costs in terms of aircraft, ships and submarines. The following day, the Italians sent a single reconnaissance aircraft to assess the damage. It was shot down. Malta had been in this situation before when the Turks had lain siege 1565 to what had become the home of the Knights of St. John. Supported by the British, they had risen against the French in 1798 and overthrown them. As the authorities in London began to realise that the island could take what the Regia Aeronautica could throw at it, so they began to look to strengthen it not only for defensive but also for offensive action. Hurricane and Swordfish aircraft were despatched, the former to take an increasing toll of the raiders and the latter of shipping. Wellington bombers were added in September to hammer enemy ports and once more the island became a fortress, one that would

Mussolini announcing the declaration of war in Rome. In 1919 Mussolini founded the *Fasci di Combattimento*, forerunner of the Fascist Party, and following the legendary March on Rome was invited to form the government by King Victor Emmanuel III in 1922. In 1928 he became absolute dictator and his decision to invade Abyssinia in 1935 destroyed the League of Nations and Italy lost its few remaining ties with Western Europe. (Australian War Memorial – PO2018.011)

The raid on Taranto was carried out by Fairey Swordfish aircraft of the Fleet Air Arm – the 'Goldfish Gang' as they were known affectionately to their naval colleagues. These puny, obsolete aircraft, armed with 18in. (46mm) torpedoes that they dropped from less than 100 feet (30m) and within 1,000 yards (910m) of their targets, sank three Italian battleships; the *Italia*, *Conti di Cavour*, and *Caio Dulio*, and damaged the cruiser *Trento* and two destroyers. (IWM – A3536)

face great strain and hardship over the next three years, but would give as good as she got.

In Egypt the declaration of war found the armoured cars of the 11th Hussars (Prince Albert's Own) under Lieutenant-Colonel John Combe lying close by the frontier. With instructions to raise hell, they immediately crossed the fence of barbed wire built by Italian engineers along the 400-mile (644km) border. In a series of dashing hit-and-run raids, they attacked forts and shot up transport columns, capturing bewildered soldiers whom nobody had bothered to inform about Mussolini's declaration. By dawn on 12 June, all their patrols had returned, bringing with them 70 prisoners and having suffered no casualties. More importantly, they had established a moral superiority over the Italians.

Encouraged by this start, plans were made to assault Forts Maddalena and Capuzzo; the attacks were launched on 14 June. Joined by elements of 4th Armoured Brigade commanded by Brigadier J. R. L. 'Blood' Caunter (named after his favourite exhortation 'Buckets of Blood!') and 1st Battalion, King's Royal Rifle Corps, Fort Maddalena fell without a shot being fired, having already been abandoned by all but 18 of the garrison. Fort Capuzzo offered some small resistance, but its 226 men also surrendered without bloodshed. Of some significance was the result of an encounter with six Italian Fiat-Ansaldo L3 Tankettes. These were engaged with a Boyes anti-tank rifle, which knocked one out immediately while the others ran 'like a lot of little pigs'.

Two days later, two troops of 11 H were 'swanning around' between Sidi Omar and Fort Capuzzo when one troop encountered an Italian column of 12 L3s and 30 lorries, apparently on their way to re-garrison the fort. At almost the same time, the second troop reported another column of 17 L3s and 40 lorries heading to meet the first. Although the squadron commander ordered them to withdraw, the two troops had eagerly charged forward to engage the enemy. During a brisk skirmish, they managed to knock out three of the L3s before retiring behind a slight rise when the column produced a field gun. Combe quickly gathered all the available reserves, including a mixed squadron of Light and Cruiser tanks from 7th Queen's Own Hussars, and an anti-tank troop of the Royal Horse Artillery from 4 Armd Bde, and rushed to join the action. When he arrived at the rise, he was staggered to see the column (the second one never appeared) some three miles away on a completely open plain, formed up in square as if fighting colonial tribesmen.

Unsure if the Italians had more artillery, Combe sent forward some of the tanks who were fired at by the single gun and charged by the L3s. These were knocked out with one shot each, whereupon the tanks circled the square in Red Indian fashion, shooting up the unprotected infantry and lorries. They made two complete circuits before the Italians revealed hidden guns at each corner. After a bitter but intense firefight in which the gallant gun detachments were shot down to a man, the square broke, only to be promptly rounded up. Barely 100 men and a dozen lorries were left to make the sad journey into captivity. Thus ended the 'Battle' of Nezuet Ghirba. Among the dead was *Colonello* D'Avanso whose pocket yielded his orders. They were to 'destroy enemy elements which have infiltrated across the frontier, and give the British the impression of our decision, ability and will to resist'.

The free-wheeling continued until the end of July, by which time the Italians were deploying heavy all-arms columns supported from the air. Steadily, their strength was increasing, including support from a few M11/39 tanks and invariably from their efficient and brave artillery. At sea, the Royal Navy shelled a flotilla of minesweepers in Tobruk harbour,

Malta was absolutely vital to British strategy in the Mediterranean and was subjected to ferocious air attack from 11 June. Cunningham could do very little to interfere with Italian convoys sailing from Italy to Libya until the defences could be strengthened. Air Commodore F. H. M. Maynard, AOC Malta, had sadly concluded that the four fighter squadrons earmarked for the island's defence would never materialise, but help was at hand. (Imperial War Museum – G(M)3407)

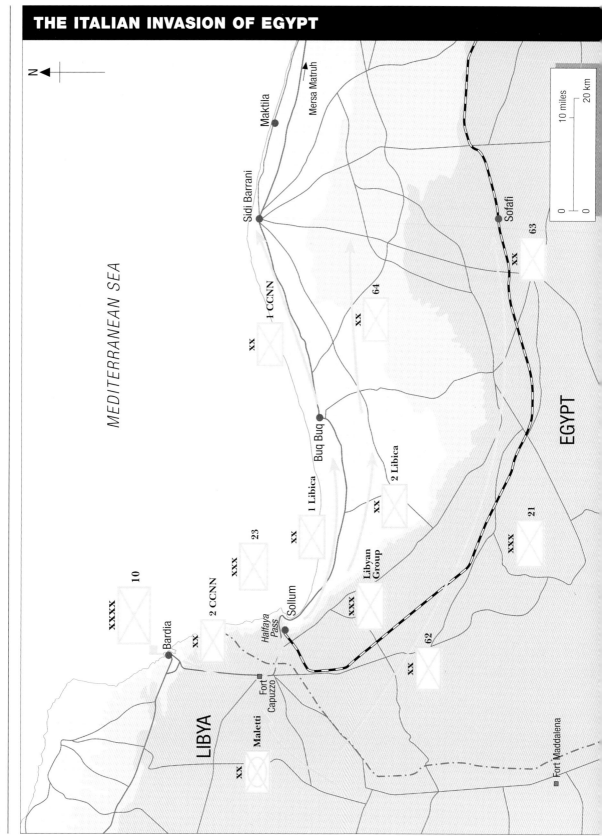

an action admired by an 11 H patrol on the beach, only 100 miles (161 km) behind enemy lines! Apart from continuous anti-submarine operations, the RN encountered no surface opposition and bombarded Bardia on 21 June. The Italians retaliated with night air-raids on Alexandria and Aboukir. A week later they attacked Royal Air Force bases at Sidi Barrani and Mersa Matruh, whose Gladiator fighters matched the opposing Fiats. But they failed to launch an effective air campaign, either against the RAF or against vulnerable Allied shipping.

Desert conditions impose considerable wear and tear on equipment, especially on vehicles, and in mid-August, 4 Armd Bde was withdrawn and replaced by 7th Armoured Brigade and 7th Armoured Division's Support Group under Brigadier W. H. E. 'Strafer' Gott. His orders were to maintain observation and impose delay with his two infantry battalions, artillery regiment and supporting elements. 11 H were ordered to reduce their activities and rest half their number. Neither side had made any territorial acquisitions but the opportunity had been there for the testing of equipment, techniques and, most importantly, of men. Both sides suffered from technical deficiencies but where the Italians had the benefit of superior numbers, the British undoubtedly held a professional and moral advantage. The first three months of the campaign saw the British inflict 3,500 casualties upon the Italians for the loss of just 150.

Although he had assured Adolf Hitler that preparations were complete for an invasion of Egypt on 17 July, Mussolini was still being fobbed off by his commanders six weeks later. Finally, on 7 September he lost his patience and issued an ultimatum to his commander in Libya, *Maresciallo* Rodolfo Graziani – either invade or be sacked. Plagued by a chronic shortage of transport, Graziani quickly modified his plan and began preliminary moves on the 9th. Under heavy air attack and worried by rumours of huge British armoured forces operating south of the escarpment, he changed his plans again and made his main effort along the coast. Thus, the Italians finally crossed the frontier in strength on 13 September. Heralded by bombardments of empty desert, a cautious advance down the Halfaya Pass (nicknamed, unsurprisingly, 'Hellfire' Pass by the British) was begun towards the tiny port of Sollum, in motor columns as if on parade.

The sole British presence was a platoon of 3rd Bn, Coldstream Guards who quietly slipped away while the RHA and RAF caused havoc and carnage amongst the advancing Italians. The next day, the guns of the RHA pounded the plodding columns until it was time to retire, covered by 3 Coldm Gds, to the next position. The process was repeated until the Italians finally reached Sidi Barrani. Here, after 60 miles (97km) and still barely half way to the main British defensive position, they stopped. Continually watched by 11 H, Graziani refused to advance another step without reinforcements, particularly guns and tanks as well as supplies. Instead, they began work to establish a new line of fortified camps. Weeks passed.

During the quiet, Mussolini decided to 'occupy' Greece on 28 October. This was prompted by a fit of pique at not having been informed beforehand of the German occupation of Romania. The Greeks, however, had no intention of being occupied: humiliating defeat was repeatedly administered to the invaders. Reinforcements would not be available for Egypt.

Meanwhile, 'Strafer' Gott was responsible for dominating the 70 miles (113km) between the two armies, and protecting 11 H which remained the only reconnaissance force available to observe the enemy in his new camps. Since details of the camps were sparse, and both the camps themselves and the tempting gaps between them needed close scrutiny if they were to be attacked successfully, small all-arms groups known as 'Jock Columns' were instituted to protect the information gatherers and to dominate no man's land. Named after Lt-Col (later Maj-Gen) J. C. 'Jock' Campbell RHA, they included one or two motorised companies of infantry, engineers and anti-tank artillery, with the armoured cars and a few tanks and appropriate support vehicles, but relied for their real hitting power on their two troops of 25-pounder guns.

Two such columns were operating by October, lifting mines, harassing communications and rear areas, but other groupings were also involved in raids. One such raid on 23 October, by 2nd Bn, Queen's Own Cameron Highlanders and 8th King's Royal Irish Hussars on the Maktila Camp, found the garrison ready and waiting for them. Fortunately, they managed to extricate themselves without serious loss but a very valuable lesson had been learned. The raid was very obviously compromised by café gossip in Cairo, home to many Italian nationals and innumerable spies, and future operations could not afford such carelessness. The Italians, however, seemed content that their camps were proof against direct attack and remained inside them strengthening their defences. Meanwhile, they surrendered no man's land and the initiative to the British.

Despite the apparent reduction of Italian effort to invade Greece, the effect on the British commanders in the Middle East was to add another burden to their considerable responsibilities, when Churchill offered

Eight Sea-Gladiators were in Malta in packing cases which the Navy agreed Maynard could use. Four were uncrated and assembled, and volunteer pilots called for. Scratch ground crews were assembled and one aircraft was placed in reserve. After some training, they took to the air and were soon christened *Faith*, *Hope*, and *Charity*. Alone, they took on raid after raid until four Hurricanes arrived at the end of July. This is *Faith*, piloted by Flt Lt George Burges. (IWM – MH3992)

Matruh, Alexandria and Suez' – an Italian propaganda poster shows the way. In North Africa, there could be rich pickings for a great new 'Roman Empire'. In the whole of the Middle East, the British, facing a difficult enough policing operation, could barely muster 50,000 troops. With 200,000 men in Libya, and another 250,000 menacing British East Africa from Abyssinia and Eritrea, Mussolini's talk of the Mediterranean as a 'Mare Nostrum' did not seem such an idle boast. (TM – 3230/B1)

the Greeks immediate assistance. At sea, the RN having had the best of early exchanges with their Italian counterparts were able to attack troop concentrations along the coast from as early as August. The gunboat HMS *Ladybird* entered Bardia harbour and calmly selected targets by searchlight, destroying any guns foolish enough to reply. In the air, the Desert Air Force provided air recce in support of both the army and navy and bombed distant targets like Tobruk, while operating fighter cover with its Gloster Gladiators. Air Chief Marshal Sir Arthur Longmore used his single available Hurricane to good effect, sending it hither and yon to bluff the Italians into thinking it was but one of many. Nevertheless, the Regia Aeronautica fought back hard, bombing Alexandria and the vital island of Malta, and enjoying technical superiority for a while until Hurricane fighters arrived in significant numbers.

OPPOSING COMMANDERS

Italian Commanders

On 28 June, Italian anti-aircraft gunners in Tobruk shot down their commander-in-chief, Maresciallo Italo Balbo, as he was returning from Rome. Although a British air raid was taking place at the time and it was almost certainly accidental, rumours circulated that his death had been ordered by Mussolini, who later commented that Balbo was 'the only one capable of killing me'. The RAF dropped a note of regret and a wreath that was gratefully acknowledged and Italy had lost probably its best commander. His replacement was Maresciallo Rodolfo 'Lucky' Graziani. Also nicknamed 'The Butcher of the Desert' after the savagery with which he slaughtered the Senussi Arabs during a rebellion in the early 1930s, he was regarded as Italy's best desert fighter. In 1936, he was made Viceroy of Ethiopia but his brutal efforts to secure Italian control became so outrageous that he was replaced in 1937 by the Duke of Aosta. In command of the Army of the Po at the outbreak of war, Graziani was also in charge of the abortive invasion of southern France.

Maresciallo Rodolfo Graziani had quite a reputation for élan within the armed forces following the Senussi campaign and the invasion of Abyssinia in 1935. When made Viceroy of Ethiopia, he was also made Maresciallo d'Italia and Marchese di Neghelli. But when he proved incompetent and cowardly against the British, Mussolini declared that 'here is another man with whom I cannot get angry, because I despise him'. (TM – 3454/B6)

Realising the difficulties presented by desert operations, and obsessed with the logistic complications, he resisted all of Mussolini's entreaties to assume the offensive despite his overwhelming numerical superiority. He expressed a prophetic pessimism to the Foreign Minister, Count Ciano: 'The water supply is entirely insufficient. We move towards a defeat, which in the desert, must inevitably develop into total disaster.' It was hardly an attitude conducive to inspiring his troops to a glorious offensive and the early operations did nothing for his confidence.

In Cyrenaica, the Tenth Army was commanded initially by Generale Mario Berti. Berti was absent on sick leave when the British offensive began; the commander of Tripolitania's Fifth Army, Generale Italo Gariboldi, was acting as his deputy. He would in due course replace Graziani following the denouement at Beda Fomm. It would be left to the most colourful of the Italian commanders to make the surrender. Generale Annibale Bergonzoli was known as Barba Elletrica because of his flaming red beard, an acclaim won during the Spanish Civil War but devalued by the British who translated it as 'Electric Whiskers'. In spite of this he was a dignified figure and was highly regarded at the outset of the war as a tough, austere field commander. He commanded the garrisons in Bardia and subsequently Tobruk, having abandoned four divisional commanders and escaped the former on foot.

British Commanders

On 2 August 1939, General Sir Archibald Wavell was appointed Commander-in-Chief to the newly created Middle East Command. Wavell joined the Black Watch (Royal Highland Regiment) in 1901, and was a noted scholar with a distinguished record. In his new post he faced

On 23 December, Generale Giuseppe Tellera took over Tenth Army from Gariboldi, and he commanded it for the remainder of the campaign until he was captured, mortally wounded, with his entire staff at the final battle. (TM – 3454/C3)

colossal difficulties in the face of overwhelming odds, not least of which was his relationship with the Prime Minister, Winston Churchill. Churchill described Wavell as 'a good, average colonel' after a visit to London in August 1940. Churchill's gross underestimation of Wavell was made worse by his constantly seeking to interfere with Wavell's detailed work, and at one point Wavell even considered resigning. Fortunately, 'The Chief' as he was popularly known did not, and this was just as well for he went on to perform prodigious feats of generalship, vastly outnumbered everywhere, and controlling simultaneous campaigns that eventually encompassed 14 territories and countries on three continents.

Lieutenant-General Sir Henry Maitland Wilson was General Officer Commanding, British Troops Egypt. The good-natured 'Jumbo' Wilson was an essential cog in the machinery since he was responsible for the difficult task of bringing troops into the theatre, accommodating, feeding and watering them, while at the same time planning for various operations. In Lt-Gen Richard O'Connor, GOC, Western Desert Force, Wavell had a field commander of outstanding talent: quick-witted (and with a grasp of detail that matched his own) cool under pressure and able to impart that serenity to his subordinates, and always appearing at the right place, at the right time, to exert his will on the battle. His regiment was The Cameronians (Scottish Rifles) and he shared the instinctive grasp of mobile mechanised warfare displayed by other light infantry officers, most notably Heinz Guderian.

Throughout the campaign, the Army received excellent support from the RAF under the command of Air Chief Marshal Sir Arthur Longmore KCB DSO, who skilfully preserved his dwindling reserves to keep up the pressure on the Regia Aeronautica. Australian born Longmore was 55 in 1940 and became AOC-in-C in May. Sir Maurice Dean said he was 'intelligent, polished, highly competent and imperturbable, just the man for stormy days in 1940'. Uncertain of the exact limits of his sphere of command, Longmore asked for

Wavell, Longmore and Cunningham: Australian-born Air Chief Marshal Sir Arthur Longmore KCB DSO was 55 in 1940 and became AOC-in-C in May. 'Intelligent, polished, highly competent and imperturbable, just the man for stormy days in 1940', he had the happy gift for 'bluffing a full house with a couple of pairs'. Admiral of the Fleet Sir Andrew Cunningham was probably the outstanding British naval commander of the war. Highly competent and aggressive, he was exactly the right man for the job. (AWM – 006456)

Despite 'Jumbo' Wilson's apparently placid nature, this large imposing man was an experienced soldier who eventually became a Field Marshal and Supreme Allied Commander, Mediterranean Theatre. John Connell says he proved to be 'shrewd, clear-headed and massively calm in manner' but Ronald Lewin says that his 'absence of originality or scintillation enabled him to float upward unimpeded.' Either way, his role in Compass became increasingly redundant. (IWM – E2008)

O'Connor was not a student of the theories of blitzkrieg, but regarded his tactics as being no more than the application of logic, commenting that 'had they been incorrect, the Italians would have fought a great deal better, slowed up our advance and given us much heavier casualties. Surprise in every form was what the Italians disliked.' For his exploits in the campaign, he was made a Knight Commander of the Bath. (IWM – E1899)

clarification, which he received on 11 June: 'He was to command "all RAF units stationed or operating in Egypt, Palestine, Trans-Jordan, East Africa, Aden and Somaliland, Iraq and adjacent territories, Cyprus, Turkey, Balkans, Mediterranean Sea, Red Sea, Persian Gulf" – an area of some 4 million square miles with some 29 squadrons, chiefly of assorted antiques. Distance, dust and sand all placed enormous strain on maintenance schedules and Churchill's lack of understanding or sympathy for these requirements made Longmore's task all the more difficult. Clearly he would need his 'happy gift for bluffing a full house with a couple of pairs'. No. 202 Gp comprised six squadrons under Air Commodore Raymond Collishaw DSO OBE DSC DFC, a Canadian and third highest scoring ace of WWI. From the opening day, 11 June, the RAF established a moral ascendancy over the Regia Aeronautica by aggressive tactics, even risking losses it could ill afford.

The Royal Navy under the command of 'the outstanding British naval leader of the war', Admiral Sir Andrew Browne Cunningham ('ABC'), despite facing the 'heaviest odds in British naval history' was also able to provide valuable support to land operations. Having become Commander-in-Chief, Mediterranean Station in June 1939, Cunningham's main concern was the protection of convoys through the Mediterranean for both Egypt and Malta, the importance of which he fully appreciated. During the later part of the campaign when increasing demands were being made of the fleet to support operations in both Cyrenaica and Greece, he never faltered. 'Stick it out' he signalled towards the end of the latter ill-fated venture, 'we must never let the Army down'. They never did, providing devastating bombardments and later helping to ease the transport burden along the coast.

OPPOSING ARMIES

Italian Forces

Although it had been on a war footing for five years, engaged with various, poorly armed colonial enemies, the *Regio Esercito* (Italian Army) was clearly not ready to fight a modern war. Full mobilisation had been declared on 10 May 1940 and forces overseas were reinforced. But although there was no shortage of the sturdy peasant stock that made up the bulk of the army, technical skills and experienced leaders were few: the military ability of the officer corps was inadequate. Following a reorganisation in 1938, 'binary' divisions were created with just two infantry regiments. These usually adopted the name of the corresponding brigade (of paired regiments dating originally to the Kingdom of Sardinia in 1815) but were also numbered, and amounted to perhaps 13,000 men – although many were mere skeletons providing Mussolini with the illusion of military strength – manpower was plentiful but equipment was not. Apart from the specialist infantry such as the Bersaglieri, the infantry was of poor quality, both in terms of training and leadership.

In addition, the Fascist Militia (*Milizia Volontaria par la Sicurrezza Nazionale* – MVSN), known as Blackshirts (*Camicie Ne* – CCNN), provided legions (regiments) that were supposedly incorporated into the infantry divisions in March 1940, and also formed a number of CCNN divisions from colonists in Libya. This organisation rewarded political enthusiasm rather than military efficiency with corresponding results. Raised within Libya itself was the *Regio Corpo di Truppe Libiche* (Royal Corps of Libyan Troops) comprising two divisions organised along similar lines to metropolitan formations but poorly equipped, and comprising 900 Italian and 6,500 native troops. A third ad hoc division, *Gruppo Malletti*, named after its commander, was formed around an infantry regiment and a tank group. Further native troops were maintained in the Sahara, guarding principal oases and outposts, and included

The L3 or CV3 (*Carro Veloce* – fast tank) was designed for infantry support, particularly in mountainous areas. It performed this function adequately in Abyssinia, but was utterly useless in any other situation. Armed with either only a single 6mm or two 8mm machine-guns, the 13.5mm of armour meant it was little more than a death trap for its two-man crew. (TM – 3186/D1)

Bersaglieri (sharpshooters), easily recognisable by the plume of cockerel feathers that adorns their head-dress to this day, were formed in 1835 by Marquis Luciano de La Marmora. By 1859 there were ten battalions with a reputation for bravery that was enhanced during the First World War. In Libya, their organisation was flexible and many motorcycle companies were formed in addition to organic units.

The 1924-pattern Rolls-Royce armoured car was one of two types operated by 11 H. With a maximum speed of 45mph (72km/h), the normal armament of a Vickers machine-gun was replaced by a 14mm Boys anti-tank rifle and a Bren light machine-gun. The frontier wire was breached by pushing slowly until it gave way under the pressure, a technique practised on a specially constructed replica. (IWM – E178)

garrison machine-gun companies, a camel battalion and motorised companies (*Compagnia Sahariana*). The *Guardia alla Frontiera* (GaF – Frontier Guards) were organised the same way as in Italy including infantry, artillery and engineers and was responsible for lines of communication as well as frontiers. Guard sectors included Bardia, Tobruk and Tripoli.

When, in due course, they captured Italian equipment, the Commonwealth troops were less than impressed. The rifles and machine-guns certainly did not compare with their own. There was a wide variety of small arms in use ranging from 6.5–7.35mm calibre, and the grenades seemed to pose no threat beyond about 6 feet. Even the artillery seemed to pack little punch and it was often supplemented by 81mm mortars organised in battalions at divisional level. Although the 47mm anti-tank gun was reasonable by contemporary standards, much of the field artillery was obsolescent.

Apart from being equipped with the useless L3s, the Italians lacked an effective medium tank and while the M13/40 was a marginal improvement on the M11/39, neither was available in great numbers. To further confuse matters, more than half of their armour was operated by the infantry branch, with battalions initially parcelled out to the divisions. Following the opening engagements, all were put under command of Generale Valentino Babini's *Commando Carri Armati dell Libia* (Libyan Tank Command) on 28 August. In November, a special armoured brigade was formed initially comprising 57 M13/40 medium tanks from III and V Bns, three battalions of Bersaglieri, an armoured car squadron, two motorised anti-tank batteries, artillery regiment, engineer company, two lorry companies and administrative support. Total Italian tank strength was 145 M13/40s (III, V, VI and XXI Bns), 70 M11/39s (I and II Bns) and 339 L3 tankettes.

On 10 June 1940, there were two Italian armies in Libya. The Fifth in Tripolitania covered the French possessions to the west, and the Tenth faced the British in Cyrenaica. With the fall of France, the Tenth Army was reinforced with troops from the Fifth so that the British would be far outnumbered. A major drawback, however, was that most of the divisional transport was horse-drawn, despite the divisions deployed to Libya being designated *Autotrasportibile tipo Africa Settentriole* and therefore, supposedly fully motorised. The Italians possessed more motor transport than the German Army in 1940, but it was to be provided to these formations from central command resources, which were hopelessly inadequate. In due course, large quantities of vehicles would fall into British hands, enabling them to press onwards.

The Italian Army's gross deficiencies were not limited to transport and armour; there were not enough anti-tank and anti-aircraft guns. Added to the inadequacies of their intelligence service, which vastly overestimated British strength throughout the campaign, the subsequent reputation of the Italian as a fighting soldier appears unfair. It has overlooked the handicaps he fought under, and ignored the gallantry displayed, especially by the artillery who often fought until shot down around their guns. After all, it takes greater courage to go into battle with bad equipment and an inept doctrine, than full of confidence in one's military institutions.

The Regia Aeronautica outnumbered the RAF as well. In the Mediterranean and Middle East theatre, they deployed around 2,600 front-line aircraft and had easier routes for reinforcement. But they too suffered from chronic shortages; of spare parts, fuel and reserves. This situation was later exacerbated by the land and sea blockade of Libya, added to which the maintenance organisation was poor. Their aircraft were respected, but the British pilots expected to have the upper hand. In May 1940, the British estimated that the Italians had 340 aircraft in Libya, with about half based in Cyrenaica facing the British. In fact there were 542 of which only 306 were operational.

Generally, the ships of the Regia Marina were well-built and well-armed although some required modernisation. A particular weakness, partly offset by the Regia Aeronautica, was a lack of aircraft carriers. The main fleet was based at Taranto, but this was nullified by the daring raid by Swordfish torpedo bombers of the Fleet Air Arm in November 1940. This raid sank three battleships and damaged a cruiser and two destroyers for the loss of two aircraft and four aircrew. A singular threat was posed by the submarine fleet, but this too was unprepared for war and within a short time, so many had been sunk that numbers on patrol were severely reduced.

Libya was the name given to the Italian colony comprising the three territories bordering the Mediterranean, dating back to its conquest in 1912. Only the fertile coast in Cyrenaica was extensively settled by colonists, but wherever they went, the Italians built monuments. The grandiose 'Arch of Fileni' between El Agheila and Sirte (approximately halfway between Tripoli and Egypt) became known as 'Marble Arch' to the British. (TM – 2776/D2)

British and Commonwealth Forces

In the Middle East, all Churchill's grandiose talk of the 'Army of the Nile' did nothing to hide British deficiency. There were only 36,000 men in Egypt, a nominally independent and neutral country in which British troops had permission to operate in defence of the Suez Canal. 20-year-old King Farouk of Egypt and his people were far from enthusiastic about the British presence, and the king surrounded himself with Italian courtiers. Pro-Axis sympathies among the government and army were a cause for great concern to the British until the final defeat of the Axis at El Alamein late in 1942. Egypt's own forces were stretched in providing internal security and had to be supple-mented by British forces who were also stretched to provide internal security for Palestine.

At least the standard of training and preparation for desert operations was already high, thanks to Wavell. In the case of 7th Armoured Division, this was particularly due to Major-General Percy Hobart. Hobart had made himself deeply unpopular in the British Army before the war by his seemingly unfettered enthusiasm for the tank. Nevertheless he built up the Mobile Division (as it was then known) and taught his men the complexities of desert operations – navigation being most important. Unfortunately, after a disagreement with Wilson he was replaced, and further changes were made to the division to create the two armoured brigades and the support group. The designation 7th Armoured Division was made on 11 June 1940 and at that time, it was the only complete formation available for active operations.

In due course, 4th Indian Division was brought up to strength and Australians and New Zealanders slowly began to arrive, the first being 6th Australian Division. These Commonwealth divisions were organised along British lines, with a divisional headquarters commanding three brigades each of three infantry battalions, plus three field artillery regiments, a cavalry regiment for medium reconnaissance duties and supporting engineers and services. The Indian infantry were long-service Regulars, most of the officers being British. The Aussies were all volunteers, full of spirit and thoroughly determined to live up to their fathers' fighting reputation, forged in the same desert sands and in the mud of Flanders during the First World War.

All the British forces were armed with the reliable Short Magazine Lee-Enfield (SMLE) .303in. rifle that had demonstrated such worth in the First World War. They also had the new Bren light machine-gun and 76mm mortars to increase their fire-power. Furthermore, among the supporting arms was the trusty Vickers medium machine-gun, operated by separate battalions. Most of the field artillery was equipped with the excellent new 25-pdr. gun/howitzer together with 4.5in. (114mm) and 6in. (150mm) medium artillery, obsolescent but packing greater punch than the Italian counterparts. Most importantly, all transport was mechanised and while there was never enough of it, it was scaled far more plentifully than that of the Italians.

Armour support included the Universal Carrier in a variety of roles (each infantry battalion had at least one platoon and it equipped the divisional cavalry regiments) and the Vickers Light Tank Mark VI which equipped divisional cavalry and some of 7 Armd Div's regiments.

The principal British defence line was constructed at Mersa Matruh some 60 miles (97km) east of the limit of the Italian invasion of Egypt at Sidi Barrani. It was held with four British battalions and built with whatever materials were available, including this turret from an old Vickers Medium tank. Its real strength however, was the mobile presence of 7 Armd Div in its rear. (IWM – E828)

Although each of these vehicles was reasonably fast, they were very lightly armoured and useful only for recce and support tasks. The former was usually armed with a Boys anti-tank rifle and a Bren, the latter with Vickers .5in. and .303in. machine-guns and thus had no anti-armour capability. The other armoured regiments in 7 Armd Div were equipped with various marks of Cruiser tanks. These were slightly better armoured and were armed with machine-guns and a 40mm 2-pdr. gun which meant they could engage Italian armour, but the 2-pdr. only fired solid shot, so it was of limited value against soft targets. The regiments within 7 Armd Div took to swapping squadrons so that each would have at least one equipped with either Lights or Cruisers. Most significant were the Matildas operated by 7th Bn, Royal Tank Regiment. These were designed for direct support of infantry and created an enormous shock, being virtually impregnable.

On assuming command of the RAF in the Mediterranean and Middle East, Longmore had found no modern fighters or long-range bombers. He too was faced with a great shortage of spares and other equipment and immediately set about increasing his resources. In August 1940, a start was made to rearm with modern types, but by the end of the year he possessed only 87 Hurricane fighters, 85 Blenheim IVs and 41 Wellington bombers. It took 70 days for reinforcements to reach Egypt via the Cape. In July 1940, an advanced party of technicians was sent to Takoradi in the Gold Coast (Ghana) to begin work on the installations necessary to open the new trans-Africa route for reinforcement traffic designed to handle up to 140 aircraft per month. So well did they work that the first reinforcement flight took off on 20 September flying via Fort Lamy (won for the Free French by General Philippe Leclerc on 29 August). By the end of October 1943, over 5,000 aircraft had been despatched to Egypt via the Takoradi Route. Only at sea and especially after Taranto did the British enjoy marked superiority, largely thanks to their aircraft carrier capability. This was reinforced by the moral inferiority of the Italians whose staff reported even before hostilities began, that British naval power in the Mediterranean 'compared with ours cannot be described other than of crushing superiority'.

The *Apology* convoy travelling via the Cape of Good Hope brought three precious armoured regiments from Britain: 3rd The King's Own Hussars with light tanks, 2 RTR with cruisers and 7 RTR with Matildas. This 2 RTR A13 Cruiser still shows its 1 Armd Div markings while the crewman wears kit very obviously issued in the UK. The 'roll-up' shorts were hated and would be rapidly discarded. The convoy also brought much-needed anti-tank and anti-aircraft guns. (IWM – E674)

ITALIAN FORCES

Maresciallo Rodolfo Graziani

Note: This is an approximate order of battle at the time of Compass and once operations commenced, organisation was very much on an ad hoc basis due to its vast losses.

TENTH ARMY

Generale d'Armata Italo Gariboldi
(*Generale d'Armata* Giuseppe Tellera from 23.12.40)
(HQ Bardia)
Tenth Army troops
 10th and 12th Bersaglieri Regiments,
 12th, 26th and 55th Artillery Regiments
 Machine-gun battalions from 55th *Savona*, 17th *Pavia*,
  27th *Brescia* Divisions respectively plus the
  machine-gun battalion from 25th Bologna Division
  (all from Fifth Army).

Armour was controlled by Generale Valentino Babini's *Comando Carri Armati dell Libia* (Libyan Tank Command).

The *Babini* Armoured Brigade was formed at Mechili in November comprising 57 M13s (from III and V Bns.) three Bersaglieri Bns, motorcycle Bn, artillery Regt, two anti-tank Coys, Engr coy and logistic units.

XX Corps

Generale di Corpo d'Armata Ferdinando Cona
(HQ Giovanni Berta)

60th Sabratha Division (Derna)
 85th, 86th (*Verona* Bde) Infantry Regiments, 42nd Artillery Regt

Gruppo divisioni libiche (Libyan Group)
Generale di Corpo d'Armata Sebastiano Gallina
(HQ Sidi Barrani)
 2nd *Raggrupamento Carristi* (Tank Group)
  (Colonello Trivioli)
 II Bn., 4th Tank Regt, (M11/39s), IX, XX, LXI Bns. (L3s)

1st *Libica Sibelle* Division (Maktila)

2nd *Libica Pescatori* Division (Tummar)

3rd *Libica – Gruppo Malletti* (Nibeiwa)

4th *3 Gennaio* CCNN Division (at Sidi Barrani)
 250th (90th, 94th and 174th Bns),
 270th (103rd, 110th and 143rd Bns) Legions, 204th Army
  Arty Regt

XXI Corps

Generale di Corpo d'Armata Lorenzo Dalmazzo
(HQ Sofafi)
 V Bn (M13/40s), IV, LX Bns (L3s)

63rd *Cirene* Division (at Rabia/Sofafi)
 157th, 158th (Liguria Bde) Inf Regts, 45th Arty Regt

64th *Cantanzaro* Division (at Buq Buq)
 141st, 142nd Inf Regts, 203rd Arty Regt

XXII Corps

Generale di Corpo d'Armata Petassi Manella
(HQ Tobruk)
Fortress troops and artillery in Tobruk

1st *Ragruppamento Carristi* (Tank Group)
Colonello Aresca
 HQ & I Bn, 4th Tank Regt (M11/39s), XXI, (M13/40s) LXII,
  LXIII Bns (L3s)

61st *Sirte* Division (Tobruk)
 69th, 70th (*Ancona* Bde) Inf Regts, 43rd Arty Regt

XXIII Corps

Generale di Corpo d'Armata Annibale Bergonzoli
(HQ Bardia)
 Frontier Guards and Fortress troops in Bardia

1st *23 Marzo* CCNN Division (along coast between Buq Buq and Sidi Barrani)
 219th (114th, 118th, 119th Bns), 233rd (129th 133rd,
  148th Bns) Legions, 201st Army Arty Regt

2nd *28 Octobre* CCNN Division (Sollum)
 231st (71st, 81st, 102nd Bns) 203rd (103rd, 110th,
  143rd Bns) Legions, 202nd Army Arty Regt

62nd *Marmarica* Division (covering the escarpment between Sofafi and Halfaya)
 115th, 116th (Treviso Bde) Inf Regts, 44th Arty Regt

REGIA AERONAUTICA

(Aircraft as at 10.06.40)

5th Squadra Generale Felip Porro

Bombers

10 Stormo	31 x SM 79
14 Stormo	43 x SM 81, 12 x SM 79, 1 x Br 20
15 Stormo	21 x SM 81, 37 x SM 79, 3 x Br 20
33 Stormo	31 x SM 79

Fighters

2 Stormo	60 x Cr 32, 25 x Cr 42
10 Gruppo	27 x Cr 42
50 Stormo	68 x Ba 65, 17 x Ro 17, 23 Ca 310

Colonial Garrison

I Gruppo APC su Ghibli e av sahariana	32 x Ghibli
II Gruppo APC vari tipi battagli sahariana types	27 x various

Air Observation

64 Gruppo	5 x Ro 1 bis, 9 x Ro 37 bis
73 Gruppo	1 x Ro 1 bis, 8 Ro 37 bis
143 Squadron (Mare)	6 x Cant Z 501 (flying boats)
Miscellaneous	55 x various aircraft
Total	542 (306 operational)

NOTES:
- Reinforcement was a simple matter for the Italians which was just as well given the high level of inoperability. Shortages of fuel, munitions and spares were compounded by the actions of the RAF and RN blockade of Libya and the level of operability became steadily worse.
- An estimated 84 of all types were estimated to be in the Dodecanese and available for use in the eastern Mediterranean area.
- Reinforcements of aircraft included four Stormo (five Gruppo comprising Cr 32 and Cr 42 deployed to Benina, Castlebenito and Tobruk).

BRITISH AND COMMONWEALTH FORCES

General Sir Archibald Wavell

Note: This list is by no means exhaustive. Units were not always available and many support service sub-units worked in the base and line-of-communications areas; behind the frontline but nonetheless vital.

WESTERN DESERT FORCE

(XIII Corps from 01.01.41)
Lieutenant-General Richard O'Connor

Corps Troops
7th Battalion, Royal Tank Regiment (Matilda Mk II Infantry (I) Tanks)
1st and 104th (Essex Yeomanry) Regiments, Royal Horse Artillery (25-pdrs.)
51st Field Regiment (Westmoreland and Cumberland Yeomanry), Royal Artillery (25-pdrs.)
7th Medium Regiment, RA (6-inch Howitzers and 6in. guns)
64 Mediterranean Regt, RA (4.5in. guns)
37th Light Anti-Aircraft Regiment, RA (40mm Bofors anti-aircraft guns)
6th Survey Regiment, RA
5th Field Park Company, New Zealand Engineers (From Jan 1941)
2 Coys, Cyprus Regiment; Detachment, Palestine Regiment (Pioneers) (from Dec 1940)
Free French Motor Marine Company
61, 231 Coys, Royal Army Service Corps, 4th Reserve Mechanical Transport Company, New Zealand Army Service Corps;

7TH ARMOURED DIVISION
Major-General M. O'Moore Creagh

Divisional Troops
11th Hussars (Prince Albert's Own) (Rolls-Royce and Morris armoured cars)
plus No. 2 Armoured Car Squadron, Royal Air Force (Fordham armoured cars)
B Squadron, 1st King's Dragoon Guards (from February 1941) (Marmon-Herrington armoured cars)
3 RHA (2-pdr. anti-tank guns)
106 (Lancashire Hussars) RHA (37mm Bofors anti-tank guns, 20mm Breda anti-aircraft guns)
2nd (Cheshire) Field Squadron and 141 Fd Pk Sqn, Royal Engineers
7 Armd Div Signals, Royal Corps of Signals
270th Field Security Section, Intelligence Corps
7 Armd Div Provost Company, Corps of Military Police

Divisional Services
5, 58, 65 and 550 Coys., RASC; 1st Supply Issue Section, Royal Indian Army Service Corps; Divisional Workshops, Divisional Ordnance Field Park, Divisional Forward Delivery Workshop Section, 1st, 2nd and 3rd Light Repair Sections, Royal Army Ordnance Corps; 2/3rd and 3/3rd Cavalry Field Ambulance, Royal Army Medical Corps.

4th Armoured Brigade
Brigadier J. R. L. Caunter
4 Armd Bde HQ and Sigs Coy, R Sigs.
7th Queen's Own Hussars (Light tanks)
2 RTR (Cruiser tanks)
6 RTR (Cruisers)

7th Armoured Brigade
Brigadier H. E. Russell
7 Armd Bde HQ and Sigs Coy, R Sigs
3rd The King's Own Hussars (Lights)
8th King's Royal Irish Hussars (Lights)
1 RTR (Cruisers)

Support Group
Brigadier W. H. E. Gott
Sp Gp HQ and Sigs Coy, R Sigs
1st Bn, King's Royal Rifle Corps
2nd Bn, Rifle Brigade (Prince Consort's Own)
4 RHA (25-pdrs.)

4TH INDIAN DIVISION
(Until 12.12.40)
Major-General N. M. de la P. Beresford-Peirse

Divisional Troops
The Central India Horse (21st King George V's Own Horse) (carriers and Light tanks)
J Bty, 3 RHA (attached)
1, 25 and 31 Fd Regts RA (25-pdrs)
1st Bn, Royal Northumberland Fusiliers (Machine-Gun) (attached less one company)
4th Field Company (King George's Own Bengal),
12 (Queen Victoria's Own Madras),
18 (Royal Bombay)
21 Fd Coys,11 Fd Pk Coy, Sappers and MinersDiv Tps Coy, 5, 7 and 11 Ind Inf Bde Coys, RIASC,4 Ind Div Sigs, Royal Indian Corps of Signals, 14, 17 and 19 Fd Amb, Royal Indian Army Medical Corps, 4 Ind Div Provo Coy.

5th Indian Infantry Brigade
Brigadier W. L. Lloyd
5 Ind Bde HQ and Sigs Coy, R I Sigs
1st Bn, Royal Fusiliers (City of London Regiment)
3rd Bn, 1st Punjab Regiment
4th Bn (Outram's), 6th Rajputana Rifles

11th Indian Infantry Brigade
Brigadier R. A. Savory
11 Ind Bde HQ and Sigs Coy., R I Sigs.
2nd Bn, Queen's Own Cameron Highlanders
1st Bn (Wellesley's), 6th Rajputana Rifles
4th Bn, 7th Rajput Regiment

16th British Infantry Brigade (attached)
Brigadier C. E. N. Lomax
16 Bde HQ and Sigs, R Sigs.
1st Bn, Queen's Royal Regiment (West Surrey)
2nd Bn, Leicestershire Regiment
1st Bn, Argyll and Sutherland Highlanders (Princess Louise's)

Selby Force (from Mersa Matruh Garrison)
Brigadier A. R. Selby
  14 Bde HQ and Sigs, R Sigs.
  3rd Bn, Coldstream Guards
  W Company, 1 NF
  A Coy,. 1st Bn, South Staffordshire Regiment
  A Coy., 1st Bn, 22nd (Cheshire) Regiment (Machine-Gun)
Detachment, 1st Bn, Durham Light Infantry; Troop, 7 H;
Light AA Bty, RA

6TH AUSTRALIAN DIVISION
(From 12.12.40)

Major-General I. G. Mackay

Divisional Troops
  1 NF (attached from 4th Ind.Div.)
  1 Cheshire (from January, 1941)
  6th Cavalry Regiment (carriers and Light tanks)
  2/1st, 2/3rd, (25-pounders) and 2/2nd (18-pounders and
  4.5in. (114 mm) howitzers) Fd Regts

Royal Australian Artillery
  2/1st, 2/2nd and 2/8th Fd Coys, Royal Australian
    Engineers
  6 Div Supply, Ammunition and Petrol Coys., Australian
    Army Service Corps,
  2/2nd Australian Army Field Workshops, Australian Army
    Ordnance Corps
  6 Div Sigs, Royal Australian Corps of Signals
  2/1st, 2/2nd and 2/7th Fd Ambs, Australian Army
    Medical Corps
  6 Div Provo Coy, Australian Corps of Military Police

16th Australian Infantry Brigade
Brigadier A. S. Allen
  16 Bde HQ and Sigs Coy, R A Sigs
  16 A/T Coy
  2/1st, 2/2nd and 2/3rd Battalions

17th Australian Infantry Brigade
Brigadier S. G. Savige
  17 Bde HQ and Sigs Coy, R A Sigs.
  17 A/T Coy
  2/5th, 2/6th and 2/7th Bns.

19th Australian Infantry Brigade
Brigadier H. C. H. Robinson
  19 Bde HQ and Sigs Coy, R A Sigs
  19 A/T Coy
  2/4th, 2/8th and 2/11th Bns

202 GROUP, ROYAL AIR FORCE
(As at Compass)
  Air Commodore Raymond Collishaw
  45, 55, 113 (Bomber) Squadrons (Blenheims)
  33, 274 (Fighter) Sqns (Hurricanes)
  3 (Fighter) Sqn Royal Australian Air Force)
    (Gladiators/Gauntlets)
  6 (Army Co-operation) Sqn (Lysanders)
  208 (Army Co-operation) Sqn (Hurricanes/Lysanders)
  31 Air Stores Park
  Advanced Repair and Advanced Salvage Sections

Note:
Also available to Collishaw from Egypt at ACM Longmore's discretion were 37, 38 and 70 (Bomber) Sqns (Wellingtons), 216 (Bomber Transport) Sqn, (Bombays) and 230 (Coastal) Sqn (Sunderlands)

OPPOSING PLANS

Having stopped at Sidi Barrani, Graziani's intention was to consolidate and to try and rectify some of the problems facing him before continuing the advance, possibly some time in December. Principally, this involved road and defence construction since the desperate shortage of transport made effective mobile operations all but impossible. Italian intelligence was so poor that they were convinced that the British forces facing them numbered around 200,000 and Graziani railed at their inability to 'break down steel doors with our fingernails'. At the same time, they believed that British reinforcements were being funnelled to Greece and that the British were as little able to mount a desert offensive as themselves, so that Graziani permitted Berti to return to Italy on leave at the end of November. Their dispositions were fatally flawed and could not be rapidly adjusted, exposing the entire Italian army in Egypt – 'motorised on foot' as one British wag put it – to destruction in detail.

Yet even before Graziani's forces were advancing into Egypt, Wavell was beginning to think of ways to strike. He requested a study be conducted on a possible advance on Tobruk as early as 11 September, entreating the planners to avoid 'the slow ponderosity which is apt to characterise British operations'. At the same time, vital reinforcements had arrived from Britain. The *Apology* convoy which arrived on 5 September brought 7 Armd Div up to strength and also brought 50 precious Matildas, half the number then available in England at a time when the threat of invasion was at its peak. Similarly, a steady increase began in Longmore's capabilities as new aircraft, particularly Hurricanes, arrived via the Takoradi air reinforcement route from West Africa although this did not become fully operational until November.

During October, it became apparent that the Italians were building permanent field fortifications. Italian plans were further illuminated by the high quality signals intelligence now available to the British. Regia Aeronautic ciphers were 80 per cent readable throughout the campaign apart from a four week break in January by which time the army codes had also been broken. Ultra decrypts of Luftwaffe signals also made clear that no German intervention was imminent. On 20 October, Wavell sent a letter to Wilson instructing him to look into the possibility of attacking enemy positions in the triangle Sidi Barrani-Sofafi-Buq Buq. The operation would last four or five days and take 'every advantage of the element of surprise'. Wavell was also aware of the crucial need for security, and he gave the letter a tiny circulation list. Few big operations have generated so little paper work.

With the Italian invasion of Greece, there was a sudden clamour from London for the release of men and equipment to be sent to support the Greeks, when even the slightest deflection of effort would

LEFT **Gunners of 1st Anti-Aircraft Regiment, Egyptian Army. Although not officially at war with Italy, the Egyptian Army was required to provide border patrols, a contribution to the Matruh garrison, a mobile force to patrol south-west of Cairo, protection for the Alexandria–Matruh railway, nine internal security battalions and air and coast defence units for Alexandria; commitments that strained it to the utmost. (IWM – E21)**

27

have jeopardised the planned raid. Consequently, Wavell was forced to inform Anthony Eden, Secretary of State for War, who was then in the Middle East. When Eden was able to inform Churchill on 8 November, the Prime Minister was delighted, although this did not prevent him haranguing Wavell. While Churchill expected maximum exploitation with a view to the rapid release of men and materials for his projected venture in the Balkans, Wavell hoped to clear the Italians out of East Africa where they had recently expelled the British from Somaliland. Reinforcements from Egypt would be necessary for this and the only complete and trained infantry division, 4th Indian, could not achieve both tasks.

In his various instructions, Wavell emphasised mobility and the limitations imposed by restricted maintenance resources and made various tactical suggestions, although neither Wilson nor O'Connor thought highly of these. In due course, Wilson presented Wavell with O'Connor's revised plan to exploit the Enba Gap separating the Nibeiwa and Sofafi camps and to attack Nibeiwa and the Tummars from the west. Wavell had always had a taste for an unorthodox approach and he gladly approved it.

The detail of what was now known as Operation Compass was beginning to crystallize in O'Connor's imaginative mind. The attacking force would pass through the Enba Gap and 4 Ind Div would advance northwards taking the camps in detail from behind, while 7 Armd Div screened off the enemy from the south and west and a demonstration would be made from the Mersa Matruh garrison by Selby Force which would advance along the main coast road. Rather than a conventional attack with infantry and armour, the Matildas would lead the way into the camps with the infantry following up. O'Connor later wrote that the axis of attack 'depended entirely on the latest photographs indicating the presence of minefields' and that since the camps had all-round defence, any attack could be considered 'frontal'. Meanwhile, Wavell ensured that security would be backed up with deception. The impression was to be created that the Western Desert had been denuded of troops for Greece.

The logistical problem was solved by the establishment of Forward Supply Depots (FSDs). Nos. 3 and 4 with ammunition, food and fuel for five days, were set up some 30 miles in front of Mersa Matruh in no-man's land. The cover story was that these were being created in case of further Italian advances and O'Connor regularly visited the administrative units working on the build up. The 'Jock' Columns continued to screen these efforts and a sharp clash in the Enba Gap on 19 November ended with five Italian tanks destroyed and over 100 casualties with five on the British side. This stunned the Italians for the next three weeks while intensive training by the British culminated in 'Training Exercise No. 1', practising attacks on exact replicas of the camps (although none of the troops were aware of this). On the evening of 26 November, O'Connor called his senior officers together to brief them on 'Training Exercise No. 2' – the cover story for Operation Compass – only minor adjustments being necessary to the original plan.

On the same day, Wavell received a cable from Churchill asking that if the raid was successful, 'presume you have plans for exploiting it to the full'. Wavell continually played down the prospects for the raid, explaining later that 'I always meant to go as far as possible and exploit any success to the full, but I was a little apprehensive that Winston might urge me to do too much, as limitations of supply and transport never made any great appeal to him.' Two days later, Wavell sent his last written directive to Wilson, stating that 'I am not entertaining extravagant hopes for this operation, but I do wish you to make certain that if a big opportunity occurs we are prepared morally, mentally and administratively to exploit it to the full.' On 2 December, Wavell convened a conference regarding East Africa and planning the redeployment of 4 Ind Div, and on 6 December he sent a cable to London further playing down Compass. Churchill was furious. If Wavell was only playing small he wrote, 'he will have failed to rise to the height of circumstances'. It would soon become apparent if Wavell was 'only playing small'.

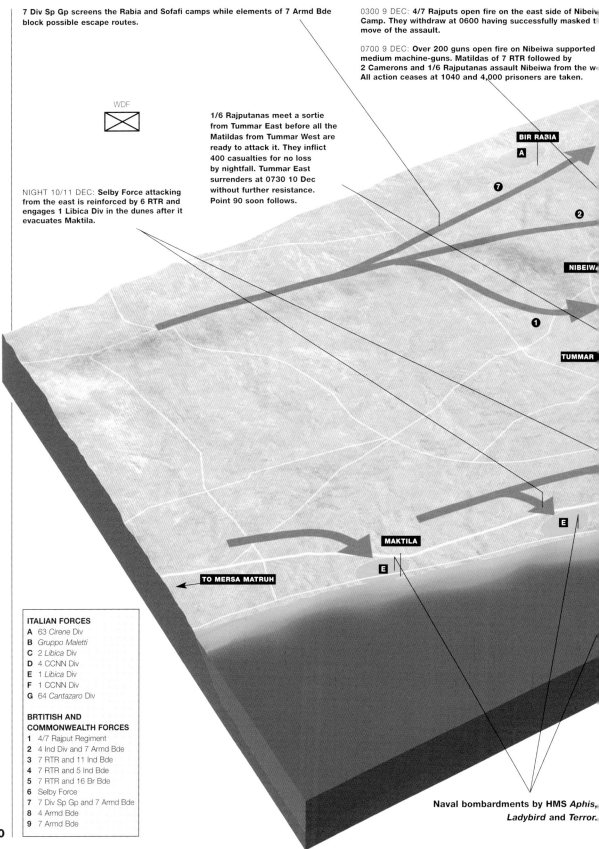

7 Div Sp Gp screens the Rabia and Sofafi camps while elements of 7 Armd Bde block possible escape routes.

0300 9 DEC: **4/7 Rajputs open fire on the east side of Nibeiw Camp. They withdraw at 0600 having successfully masked t move of the assault.**

0700 9 DEC: **Over 200 guns open fire on Nibeiwa supported medium machine-guns. Matildas of 7 RTR followed by 2 Camerons and 1/6 Rajputanas assault Nibeiwa from the w All action ceases at 1040 and 4,000 prisoners are taken.**

WDF

1/6 Rajputanas meet a sortie from Tummar East before all the Matildas from Tummar West are ready to attack it. They inflict 400 casualties for no loss by nightfall. Tummar East surrenders at 0730 10 Dec without further resistance. Point 90 soon follows.

NIGHT 10/11 DEC: **Selby Force attacking from the east is reinforced by 6 RTR and engages 1 Libica Div in the dunes after it evacuates Maktila.**

BIR RABIA

A

❼

❷

NIBEIW

❶

TUMMAR

E

MAKTILA

E

TO MERSA MATRUH

ITALIAN FORCES
A 63 *Cirene* Div
B *Gruppo Maletti*
C 2 *Libica* Div
D 4 CCNN Div
E 1 *Libica* Div
F 1 CCNN Div
G 64 *Cantazaro* Div

BRTITISH AND COMMONWEALTH FORCES
1 4/7 Rajput Regiment
2 4 Ind Div and 7 Armd Bde
3 7 RTR and 11 Ind Bde
4 7 RTR and 5 Ind Bde
5 7 RTR and 16 Br Bde
6 Selby Force
7 7 Div Sp Gp and 7 Armd Bde
8 4 Armd Bde
9 7 Armd Bde

Naval bombardments by HMS *Aphis*, *Ladybird* and *Terror*.

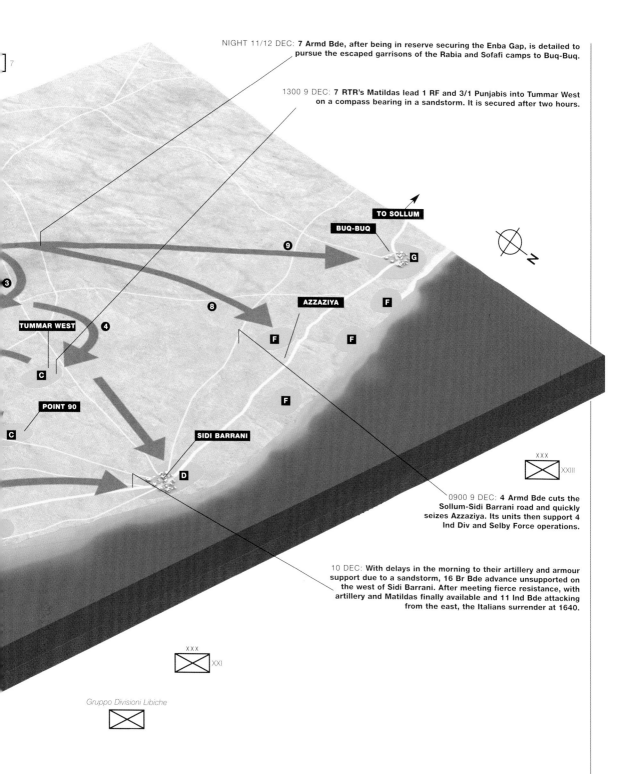

NIGHT 11/12 DEC: **7 Armd Bde**, after being in reserve securing the Enba Gap, is detailed to pursue the escaped garrisons of the Rabia and Sofafi camps to Buq-Buq.

1300 9 DEC: **7 RTR's** Matildas lead **1 RF** and **3/1 Punjabis** into Tummar West on a compass bearing in a sandstorm. It is secured after two hours.

TO SOLLUM

BUQ-BUQ

G

AZZAZIYA

F

F

F

F

TUMMAR WEST

C

POINT 90

C

SIDI BARRANI

D

0900 9 DEC: **4 Armd Bde** cuts the Sollum-Sidi Barrani road and quickly seizes Azzaziya. Its units then support 4 Ind Div and Selby Force operations.

10 DEC: With delays in the morning to their artillery and armour support due to a sandstorm, 16 Br Bde advance unsupported on the west of Sidi Barrani. After meeting fierce resistance, with artillery and Matildas finally available and 11 Ind Bde attacking from the east, the Italians surrender at 1640.

XXX
XXIII

XXX
XXI

Gruppo Divisioni Libiche

OPERATION COMPASS
9-11 DECEMBER 1940
4 Ind Div advances northwards to take the camps from behind, whilst 7 Armd Div screens off the enemy and Selby Force advances up the main coast road

THE CAMPAIGN

The Five Day Raid

The RAF had been making attacks on enemy ammunition and stores dumps, barracks and airfields at Benghazi, Derna, Tobruk and Bardia since October. But on 7 December it began concentrated attacks on Italian airfields, destroying 39 aircraft on the ground in the next two nights. During the night of 8 December, the 15in. (381mm) monitor HMS *Terror* shelled Maktila and the gunboat HMS *Ladybird* and her sister *Aphis* shelled Sidi Barrani. This increased activity was duly noted by Italian headquarters at various levels but caused no undue alarm.

Reports of vehicle movement towards the front were dismissed as being routine reliefs. A special patrol of 2nd Bn, Rifle Brigade (Prince Consort's Own) confirmed the entrance to Nibeiwa on the night 7–8 December and on this information, the final rendezvous was decided. The move forward via a concentration area called 'Piccadilly Circus' went very well, partially covered by an air raid by ancient RAF Bombays whose bombing was largely ineffective, but whose droning engines helped drown the sound of vehicles to the south. In spite of minor problems, as first light approached, the columns of hundreds of vehicles were moving steadily northwards. By 0500hrs, 11th Indian Brigade was at its RV north-west of Nibeiwa Camp.

After being shot up from the east in the night by 4th Bn, 7th Rajput Regiment which withdrew at 0600hrs, the combined corps artillery destroyed the morning routine of the Italians an hour later. Matildas of

When 3 H set off in pursuit of the enemy rearguard, they found it lining a set of sand dunes covering a salt marsh outside Buq Buq. The crust of the salt flat can be paper-thin and as the lead squadron charged across it, the tanks bogged down and were shot to pieces. In 'ten bloody minutes', 13 tanks were reduced to burning wrecks by the unbroken enemy and 10 men were killed and 13 wounded. (TM – 2257/B4)

7 RTR were moving into position opposite the north-west corner of the camp, unaware that a group of 23 M-11 tanks had leaguered there overnight. At least this proved the gap was not mined, and the M-11s were much easier to deal with. The crews were surprised before they could mount up and in no time, the Matildas were into the camp. Led by the virtually impregnable Matildas, 'the nearest thing to hell I ever saw' said an Italian army doctor afterwards, the Italians were overwhelmed as the infantry hurried in to mop up what the tanks had missed.

The camp measured 2,400 x 1,800 yards (2,200m x 1,600m). Its perimeter was largely composed of dry stone breastworks, with machine-gun posts and guns which were powerless to stop the Matildas. Apart from perimeter defence posts every 25 yards (23m), it was full of trenches, tents and stores, and the defenders of *Gruppo Maletti* fought hard for two and a half hours. Gunners clambered onto the sangar walls to throw grenades at the lumbering monsters until cut down by the hammering Besas. As one crewman said: 'The Italians may have been a pushover afterwards, but they fought like hell at Nibeiwa'. Throughout the campaign, they were to show the same selfless courage, but once the guns were silent the infantry wilted. 4,000 prisoners were taken. Some Italians simply gave up on demand but Generale Pietro Maletti, emerging from his dugout with a machine-gun in hand, was himself cut down. 7 RTR lost two men killed and five wounded.

It was all over by 1040hrs. There was no time for jubilation, particularly amongst the tank crews which immediately began their replenishment of fuel and ammunition. 5th Indian Brigade was due to attack Tummar West at 1100hrs. This was always an optimistic schedule and when 7 RTR were further delayed by a sandstorm and a minefield, which claimed seven tanks, the assault was finally set for 1335hrs and put in on a compass bearing, which thankfully put the tanks directly into the hole in the wall. Once more they fought a duel with the Italian gunners while the infantry had a much more torrid time than at Nibeiwa. The 1st Bn, Royal Fusiliers were carried to within 150 yards (137m) of the wall by the enthusiastic

Lt-Col W. G. Petherick, commanding officer (centre), and Maj A. Dawes, adjutant (right), of 3 H with the medical officer, Capt Tom Somerville OBE, MC, Croix de Guerre, RAMC (left). Somerville walked calmly among the regiment under heavy fire at Buq Buq, where he successfully performed two amputations with a jack-knife. He was awarded the Distinguished Service Order but later died in the mountains of Crete trying to avoid capture following the German invasion. (IWM – MH3849)

Captured weapons were incorporated into the Mersa Matruh defences. One of the strangest examples was this 12-pdr. mountain gun, here being operated by 1st Bn, South Staffordshire Regiment. The early operations soon demonstrated the utterly inappropriate way the Italian Army was equipped for modern mobile warfare. (IWM – E849)

New Zealander truck drivers of 4th Reserve Motor Transport Company who grabbed rifles and led the way shouting 'Come on you Pommie bastards!' Two hours' attack with bayonet and grenades yielded 2,000 more prisoners.

Refugees communicated their terror of the Matildas to Tummar East, whose fall was made easier after it launched a counter-attack against Tummar West that was swiftly destroyed in the open. A solitary Matilda was dispatched to secure its surrender, but the commander refused until it was agreed that a larger demonstration of force, backed by artillery fire (preferably not directly at the Italians), would be sufficient. However, it was already too late to do anything before nightfall. It had been a successful day at the camps. The men were amazed at what they found: perfume, manicure sets, exquisite uniforms in the officers' quarters, and beds made up with fresh linen. Even the corporals seemed to lead more luxurious lives than O'Connor in his tactical headquarters. Alan Moorehead, the Australian journalist, was astonished by what they found in the camps: '... wines from Frascati and Falerno and Chianti ... Parmesan cheeses as big as small cart-wheels ... delicate tinned tongue and tunny fish and small round tins of beef. The vegetables were of every kind ...'

Further west, a troop of 11 H had infiltrated to the coast road west of Sidi Barrani by 0900hrs followed by 7 H cutting the telephone and water supplies, and 4 Armd Bde's tanks were south-east of Buq Buq. 6 RTR had expected to meet the main enemy armour concentration but this had

drawn in towards Nibeiwa for the night. Having reached the road, 7 H were given the task of clearing the Wadi el Kharruba; the attack was quickly completed at 1140hrs, completing the isolation of all those to the east. O'Connor spent the day well forward in the wake of 7 Armd Div. He dispatched a senior liaison officer – to ensure co-ordination between the two formations – and had 8 H patrol west of the Sofafi Camps to dissuade their evacuation. While the forts were attacked, Selby Force drove west along the coast road. Unaware of their progress, O'Connor ordered 16th British Brigade to attack Sidi Barrani the following morning, while 5 Ind Bde dealt with Tummar East (it surrendered tamely at 0730hrs).

Selby Force had spent 9 December in frustrating isolation, lacking accurate information and revised directions. They kept a close watch on Maktila while the initial assaults were launched but only attempted an encirclement late in the day, when 3 Coldm Gds were advancing slowly. Overnight, the defenders from 1st Libyan Division slipped away after a repeat shelling from the RN, into a vortex formed by 4 Armd Bde pressing from the west and 16 Br Bde advancing from the south. The commander of the Libyan Group in Sidi Barrani, Generale Sebastiano Gallina, reported to Graziani that the water supply had been cut and the 'territory between Sidi Barrani and 2nd Libyan Division is infested by a mechanised army against which I have no adequate means'. On the British side, when morning came with a howling sandstorm and as yet no armour support, Brigadier C. E. N. Lomax of 16 Br Bde decided to seize the initiative.

As soon as the trucks carrying 1st Bn, Argyll and Sutherland Highlanders advanced, however, they came under accurate artillery fire and were forced to ground. On their right, 2nd Bn, Leicestershire Regiment were more fortunate; but it was the arrival of 7 RTR's 11 remaining Matildas (with 1st Bn, Queen's Royal Regiment) that enabled them to work around to the left. Combined with a choking

Probably the most famous British battleship of the war, with the finest fighting record of any ship, HMS *Warspite* displaced 30,600 tons and was armed with eight 15in. (381mm) guns. 'Great Britain,' wrote Lord Esher, 'either is, or is not, one of the great powers of the world. Her position in this respect depends solely upon sea command – and upon sea command in the Mediterranean'. (Tank Museum – 3577/B2)

Universal Carriers from 1 KRRC at Fort Capuzzo. The fort covered the approaches to Bardia and Sollum and was regarded as a key element in the Italian defensive system. Unlike the Italian L3, the carrier was just that, not a tank. It could be used as a scout vehicle, machine-gun or mortar carrier, and as a general utility vehicle. It had maximum $\frac{1}{2}$in. (12mm) armour and was usually armed with a Boys anti-tank rifle and a Bren gun. (TM – 3562/D2)

sandstorm, and British artillery countering the Italians, the battle developed from the west. Despite a short firefight between 1 A & S H and 2 Queen's at one point, they reached their objectives, while 2 Leicesters, breaking through the southern perimeter, were suddenly presented by 'a formidable body of men emerging from their trenches … as if in mass attack'. It was, in fact, 2,000 Blackshirts surrendering.

With the commitment at 1615hrs of 2 Camerons and 4th Bn, 6th Rajputana Rifles from divisional reserve, it was all over by nightfall. Gallina asked if he could address his men and emotionally thanked them for 'fighting as Fascists'. Selby Force, supported by 6 RTR, cut across from 4 Armd Bde, continued to face stiff opposition from 1 Lib Div which reduced 6 RTR to seven cruisers and six light tanks and forced them to retire. Only the addition of 4 Ind Div's artillery and pressure from the west the next morning finally persuaded the Italians of the futility of continued resistance.

Suddenly, on this morning of 11 December, O'Connor was presented with complete victory and the prospects of pursuit and exploitation. The RAF had established air superiority for the loss of 10 aircraft and the Italian forward defensive system had been crushed. Already, 20,000 prisoners, 180 guns and 60 tanks had been taken for the loss of 600 killed, wounded and missing (250 of whom came from 16 Br Bde). Point 90 surrendered at midday and with the armour bearing down on Buq Buq, the prospects were excellent. But then came bad news. O'Connor was shocked to learn that 4 Ind Div (less 16 Br Bde) was to be immediately taken away to be sent to Sudan, thus depriving him of valuable artillery and transport.

This decision was a result of the War Cabinet's deep worries over the large Italian forces in Abyssinia, although these were in reality a paper tiger. At the same time, Churchill was busily trying to tempt the Imperial

General Staff with a scheme to capture the Italian island of Pantelleria. Although Wavell promised 6 Aus Div as a replacement, this would not be available immediately and besides the pursuit, there was the business of dealing with the huge haul of prisoners and booty. Furthermore to the south-west, 7 Armd Bde had failed to prevent the evacuation of the Sofafi and Rabia camps when enveloped in thick sandstorms. That night they were sent in pursuit of the garrisons that had fled to Buq Buq.

Things continued to go badly for 7 Armd Bde They were led by a troop from 11 H which swept through Buq Buq finding it empty. Realising that the follow-up was aimed at thin air, they made calls on the radio to deflect the tanks into the flank of the enemy main body. These went unheeded as the brigade commander's tank was broken down, and Lt-Col Combe, although in an excellent position to see the battle unfolding before him, was unable to assume command before disaster befell 3rd The King's Own Hussars. As their light tanks passed Buq Buq, they entered an area of salt pans and sand dunes with Italians fleeing across them. Unfortunately, the presence of firmly emplaced artillery covering the defile was missed until it was too late and, twisting and turning to avoid the fire, 3 H found themselves bogging and stumbling to a halt.

Combe brought up artillery support and a cruiser squadron from 8 H manoeuvred to the flank. The Italians were turning to face this new threat when the explosion of an ammunition truck demoralised them into surrender. Only the Regia Aeronautica continued to resist, making a number of damaging strikes that the RAF could not prevent, their Gladiators having been withdrawn. Nevertheless, it was another massive success. A young troop commander reported to regimental headquarters: 'Have arrived at the second B in Buq Buq', and asked to supply an estimate of prisoners, another officer managed 'as far as I can see, there are twenty acres of officers and a hundred acres of men'.

In all, Compass had now yielded 38,000 prisoners, 237 guns and 73 light and medium tanks. Success had largely been achieved through surprise created by excellent security. Wavell had conspicuously attended the races with his family on 7 December followed by a dinner party for senior officers that evening. The Egyptian Prime Minister, Hussein Sirry Pasha, who took great pride in 'having sources who keep me informed of all that goes on', congratulated Wavell 'on being the first to keep a secret in Cairo'. One problem resulting from this secrecy, however, was the lack of contingency planning for the prisoners who posed enormous

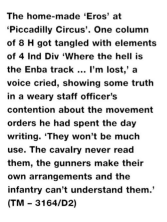

The home-made 'Eros' at 'Piccadilly Circus'. One column of 8 H got tangled with elements of 4 Ind Div 'Where the hell is the Enba track ... I'm lost,' a voice cried, showing some truth in a weary staff officer's contention about the movement orders he had spent the day writing. 'They won't be much use. The cavalry never read them, the gunners make their own arrangements and the infantry can't understand them.' (TM – 3164/D2)

BELOW **The commanding officer of 7 RTR, Lt-Col Roy Jerram, put great emphasis on the Forward Rally after a successful attack as being the place where the next attack was won. Once released by the infantry, the tanks would retire to a pre-arranged RV where the fitters brought acetylene torches to free jammed turrets, and damaged tracks and other minor repairs could be carried out. Replenishment of fuel and ammunition was also carried out before the tanks set off for their next task. (TM – 2792/B1)**

difficulties for O'Connor, especially now that he was shorn of the transport of 4 Ind Div. Nevertheless, he refused to be deflected from his task.

The RN had already bombarded the transport piling down the road from Sollum to Bardia. O'Connor hoped both would be abandoned although it was unlikely in the case of the latter. But even the little bay at Sollum with its jetty would provide much needed relief for the already hard-pressed administrative services, releasing trucks from the long haul back to Mersa Matruh. Graziani's mood was so black that he fully expected the British to sweep past Bardia and go directly for Tobruk, warning Mussolini in a doom-laden message on 12 December that he had been obliged 'to wage the war of the flea against the elephant'. Had O'Connor been aware of the depths of alarm and panic into which Graziani had sunk, he might have been tempted to press harder. But his own problems were enormous, trying to bring food, ammunition and petrol forward while moving the vast numbers of prisoners, as well as 4 Ind Div back.

LEFT **The Infantry Tank Mk II (A14) Matilda was the most powerful tank in the British inventory. Built to withstand all known anti-tank guns, it had provided a shock to Erwin Rommel's 7th Panzer Division at Arras in May. Its frontal armour was 3in. (78mm) but it only mounted a 2-pdr. gun with co-axial $^{1}/_{3}$in. (7.92mm) Besa machine-gun. It was also mechanically complicated and slow, with a flat-out maximum speed of 15mph (24km/h). (AWM – PO2038.089)**

Meanwhile, the pursuit was held at arm's length by the Italian artillery.

Only by stripping the Support Group of its vehicles was O'Connor able to push 7 Armd Bde forward, 60 miles (95km) in front of the most forward depot, to get astride the Sollum-Bardia road. On 13 December, 4 Armd Bde was able to rejoin the line, passing through a gap between Halfaya and Sidi Omar with orders to by-pass the enemy on the flanks and cut the Bardia-Tobruk road, thus completing the isolation of Bardia and possibly prompting its evacuation.

Two columns were formed for this: Combeforce, under CO 11 H, with part of that regiment, 2 RTR and two RHA batteries; and Birksforce, with the remainder of 11 H (including No. 2 Armoured Car Company, RAF, an experienced unit from Palestine) and 7 H. They advanced into a wilderness, meeting no organised opposition, merely stragglers from the various Italian formations streaming back from Egypt, and hoping for refuge in Bardia. Despite an air attack on 11 H, which inflicted some damage, the road was cut by 1000hrs. The armoured cars were particularly vulnerable to air attack and the Italians had formed a squadron specifically to hunt for them. Subjected to over 20 air attacks that day, 11 H eventually had to be withdrawn from action.

At the same time, 7 Armd Bde met determined resistance from a rearguard near Capuzzo that prevented them cutting the Sollum-Bardia road. By dawn the following day, the Italians had succeeded in getting into Bardia. 'Whether this was preventable or not I am not in a position to say,' wrote O'Connor 'I feel, however, that this question of preventing the movement of enemy columns at night must be tackled'. The inability of the British armour to operate at night was to be a recurring theme throughout the campaign, but for now, the situation had resolved itself. A powerful, if heterogeneous, force occupied Bardia; another large grouping was in the Tobruk area, and the fort at Sidi Omar held

Although designed as a medium tank, when the Cruiser Tank Mk I (A9) entered service in 1937, it was re-classified as a cruiser after the British fashion of dividing tank development between infantry (support) tanks and cruisers for general duties. Its armour was only $^{3}/_{4}$in. (14mm) maximum and its armament a 2-pdr. gun and three .303in. (8mm) Vickers machine-guns, two mounted in auxiliary turrets, giving it a crew of six when fully manned. Only 125 were ever built. (TM – 1289/C1)

'One man is much the same as another, and he is best that is trained in the severest school.' So wrote Thucydides in his Peloponnesian Wars. Training was taken very seriously by the British, and it paid off. Here, men of the Rajputana Rifles practise basic armour co-operation drills with Light tanks of 1 RTR in lieu of more substantial support. (IWM – E117)

out. With the return of Maj-Gen Micheal O'Moore Creagh to command 7 Armd Div, the task of its reduction on 16 December fell to Caunter, now back in command of 4 Armd Bde The defensive layout was very similar to the camps previously encountered but with a 'Beau Geste' style white fort in the middle.

Captain Pat Hobart commanding C Sqn, 2 RTR (Percy Hobart's nephew) described the action: 'We drove around to avoid the enemy shelling while the 25-pdrs. did their bombardment, then formed up in line, advanced at full speed on the fort in the best tradition of the "arme blanche". The enemy must have suffered pretty severely under the attentions of 4 RHA, for in we went with every gun and machine-gun firing. My orders to the Sqn were to drive straight through the perimeter, doing as much damage as possible, out the other side, then return again and rally back on the near side.' This plan was scuppered when Hobart's tank charged a stone wall and knocked off his idler wheel. His second-in-command, Captain David Wilkie, took his tank into the courtyard to find a steel-helmeted Hobart firing his revolver from the cupola. Suddenly, the 'glorious gallop' was all over and the demoralised Italians surrendered.

Over the next two weeks, naval and aerial bombardments of Bardia were intensified. On 17 December, *Aphis* steamed straight into the harbour and sank some coasters at point blank range before escaping unscathed. An attempt to repeat the feat the next day was chased off by mobile guns until out of range. *Aphis*, her sister ship *Ladybird* and *Terror* all played an important role as water carriers in addition to their aggressive duties, and wherever possible, captured Italian trucks were pressed into service to bring forward supplies. Strict instructions to 4 Ind Div on the inviolability of the FSDs had been adhered to, but O'Connor was a little annoyed to find himself having to tell its commander, Maj-Gen Noel Beresford-Peirse, to return the corps artillery units he had with him – it may have been perfectly justifiable military acquisitiveness on his part, but it also wasted time and petrol.

Bardia

The first Australian unit into action was 6th Cavalry Regiment who fought brisk actions with the garrisons of Fort Maddalena and Garn el Grein on 11 and 12 December. The main body of 16th Australian Brigade began moving up from Alexandria on 12 December followed soon afterwards by 17 Aus Bde and Divisional Headquarters, while 19 Aus Bde was held ready to move by sea direct to Bardia should the Italians evacuate, which they did not.

The Italians had fortified Bardia and Tobruk with steel and concrete. Captured plans showed an almost continuous anti-tank ditch stretching in an 18 mile (29km) arc around the little town, behind which lay a double line of underground posts consecutively numbered from south to north, linked with barbed wire. The posts in the forward line were approximately 800 yards (728m) apart, protected by their own anti-tank trench, which was later found to be concealed under thin boards. Each mounted one or two anti-tank guns and up to four machine-guns fired from concrete-sided pits connected to underground shelters. Although

Bardia was insignificant in every other respect than its 18-mile (29km) perimeter and 45,000 man garrison. Divided into two parts, one sitting atop the Escarpment and the other next to a little bay that provided only limited access for shipping. Creagh called on Jerram regarding the possible use of 7 Armd Div's cruiser tanks in the infantry support role for the assault. The sight of a Matilda that had survived 40 major hits disabused him of this notion. (AWM – 005865)

Originally, 6 Aus Div comprised 12 battalions. 16th Bde
(2/1st, 2/2nd, 2/3rd and 2/4th) was raised in New South
Wales; 17th Bde (2/5th, 2/6th, 2/7th and 2/8th) in Victoria,
while 18th Bde comprised 2/9th and two companies of
2/12th from Queensland (the remaining two companies
coming from Tasmania), 2/10th from South Australia and
2/11th from Western Australia. Here, men of 2/1st Bn wait
to assault Bardia.

the shelter provided excellent cover, the gun pits had no overhead protection and the connecting trenches also lacked a fire-step. The second line of posts ran in an arc 440 yards (400 m) behind the first but lacked an anti-tank trench and was short of wire.

O'Connor's headquarters estimated that the Italians had about 20,000 men within the perimeter, comprising its fortress troops and a vast array of stragglers from Egypt whose usefulness must have been questionable at best, while aerial photos revealed some long stone breastworks and an array of guns, estimated at 110. O'Connor suggested to the Australian commander, Maj-Gen Iven Mackay, that he mount raids covered by artillery to establish a bridgehead within the defences. O'Connor's intention was to clear Bardia with two of the Australian brigades, holding the third in readiness to move on Tobruk. Without wishing to rush the operation, he nevertheless wanted to press on.

When 16 Aus Bde, with 2/1st Field Regiment, Royal Australian Artillery in support, arrived to take over positions held by the Support Group east of the town, the division was thus strung out between Alexandria and Bardia. Mackay also took command of 16 Br Bde which held the line to the south while 7 Armd Div provided a screen to the north and west. The Aussies immediately began patrolling, both to acquire detailed information on the perimeter defences and to dominate no man's land. On a number of occasions, patrols located enemy positions and came under heavy, if ill-directed, machine-gun and artillery fire, which failed to cause a single casualty. But it was desert life, rather than enemy action, that caused greatest discomfort.

By Christmas Day, 20 casualties had been caused by bombing and 'thermos bombs' – mines resembling a small thermos flask which were armed on hitting the ground, and activated by their next movement – that the Italians had scattered over the area from the air. There was also an increased strain of administration due to the need to provide for the troops along with the burden of thousands of prisoners.

The opening of Sollum and the arrival of 50 heavy trucks from Palestine could do little to make up for the 40 per cent wastage in vehicles imposed by the harsh desert conditions and the lack of base workshop facilities.

Digging in was very difficult on the broad expanse of flat stony ground and sangars had often to be built up with rocks. The wind distributed a layer of fine yellow dust on anything not tightly wrapped up, and turned faces a yellowish-grey. Water was restricted to half a gallon per man per day – for all purposes – and hot food amounted to one meal a day involving the inevitable bully-beef. On Christmas Day, the Australians each received a rare treat: a parcel from the Australian Comforts Fund, including plum pudding, tinned cream, cake, fruit and cheese. The British received more petrol, ammunition and warnings – for the guns to conserve their shells for the main assault – and to everyone that shortages of food and water were likely to continue. On 27 December, 17 Aus Bde arrived to relieve 16 Br Bde. 2/6th Battalion took over the far right of the line and on the night 29–30 December,

advanced to positions overlooking the Wadi Muatered which cut deep into the cliff facing the sea. The Italian defences were much more lively here than opposite 16 Aus Bde, and a sortie was made towards the gun positions of 2/2nd Fd Regt, which was driven off.

O'Connor was keen to employ the remaining Matildas and on Christmas Eve had instructed Mackay to develop a plan accordingly. O'Connor promised the full use of the corps artillery (WDF became XIII Corps officially from 1 January 1941) amounting to 118 field and 42 medium guns. A plan was drawn up to concentrate between posts 45 and 47, a difficult position to locate owing to the flatness of the ground, but a route was surveyed by a patrol of 2/1st Bn who would take the lead in the assault. The operation was fixed to commence just before dawn on 3 January. Following a 25-minute bombardment, the infantry with engineer support, would break through the barbed wire and capture four Italian posts, throwing down the anti-tank ditch to enable 7 RTR to advance when it was light enough. The follow-up battalions would then push through, fanning out to the south to roll up the defences.

There was some confusion in the orders processed over the exact role of 17 Aus Bde which was to provide a demonstration to the south by 2/6th Bn. For an inexperienced formation, this was to prove unfortunate. Nevertheless, detailed preparations continued, including the procurement of 11,500 leather jerkins against the cold, wire cutters and protective gloves, which arrived only as the troops were moving towards their assembly areas. Mine tape to mark routes did not, however and the soldiers improvised with rifle-cleaning flannelette. RAF bombers had hit the fortress hard since 31 December and during 2 January the Royal Navy joined in once more, the faithful *Terror*, *Aphis* and *Ladybird*

After the main defences were penetrated, resistance crumbled. Many Italians surrendered as soon as the Aussies shouted 'lashay lay army' (*lascie le armi* – lay down your arms). 2/2nd Bn cleared the wadis to the south of the town and 2/3rd Bn climbed up towards 'upper' Bardia on the headland above the inlet. At the hospital in the town were some 500 patients and 3,000 others who had evidently gathered there for safety. (AWM – 006083)

shelling Italian positions. The Australians were about to fight their first battle of the Second World War.

The lead platoons advanced accompanied by engineer parties carrying bangalore torpedoes – 12 foot (4m) pipes packed with ammonal – as Italian artillery fire began to land, mainly behind them. Spaced at 60 yard (55m) intervals, seven parties of three engineers advanced and slid two torpedoes into the 20 foot (6m) wide fence, pushing the first through with the second. Immediately after these were blown, the infantry scrambled to their feet and rushed forward while the engineers hurried to break down the anti-tank ditch. Posts 49 and 47 were rapidly overrun and Post 46 in the second line beyond. Within half an hour Post 48 had also fallen and a second company had taken Posts 45 and 44. The two remaining companies now advanced beyond these positions as artillery began to fall along the broken wire. After a few hundred yards, they came upon a low stone wall, from which heavy but ineffective fire was coming, and took the position with grenades and bayonet, yielding some 400 prisoners.

Accustomed to the British prowling around at night, the Maletti Group had manned their perimeter positions throughout the bitterly cold desert night and been subject to several distracting false alarms. Then at 0700hrs, as breakfast was being taken, over 200 guns opened fire to ruin the start of their day. (IWM – E983)

Outside Nibeiwa was the operational strength of II Bn, 4th Tank Regiment. Although there were 70 M11/39s in theatre, they were mechanically unreliable and the regiment's I Bn was refitting near Tobruk. Essentially a development of the L3, the twin turret machine-guns were fully traversable, but the 1.5in. (37mm) gun in the hull only fired forwards. Maximum armour was 1in. (29mm), and it could manage nothing like its maximum speed of 20mph (32km/h) when moving cross-country due to its dreadful suspension. (TM – 3183/F6)

The Vickers .303in. (8mm) medium machine-gun first entered service with the British Army in 1912 and was only withdrawn in 1965. Operated here by 1st Bn, Royal Northumberland Fusiliers ('The Fighting Fifth') it was a water cooled weapon fed with 250-round belts. Besides direct fire, it was capable of indirect fire against enemy positions and suspected concentrations out to 4,500 yards (4095m), and had a rate of fire of 450rpm (although a lower rate was used in the sustained fire role). (IWM – E1812)

At 0630hrs, six tank crossings were ready and mines between them and the wire had been detected. Five minutes later, two crossings were open and the 23 Matildas of 7 RTR advanced accompanied by 2/2nd Bn smoking and singing 'South of the Border'. Passing through the gaps at around 0700hrs, they swung right along the double line of posts. To begin with the Italians fought hard, but once more were completely unable to halt the Matildas, which would fire, supported by the diggers until return fire slackened, at which point the infantry would advance (sometimes carefully and sometimes in a rush) to throw grenades into the pits and shelters. The fighting grew increasingly confused in the swirling smoke and dust, and one company was directed towards the artillery positions further in, the Italian artillerymen fighting until dead around their guns.

When 2/3rd Bn, accompanied by A Sqn, 6 Cav, moved through the wire at 0750hrs, the dust was so dense that platoon commanders could not see the platoons either side of them and navigated by compass. By 0920hrs they were on all their objectives and had linked with 2/1st Bn on their left. Italian machine-guns were found sighted at 875 or 1,094 yards (800m or 1,000m) range, unadjusted in their alarm as the Aussies, looming large in their greatcoats, took the positions with bayonet and hob-nailed boot. Strung out in a very thin line, 2/3rd Bn were now assailed by half a dozen enemy tanks who freed a group of 500 prisoners (soon returned to cowed captivity by a machine-gun burst). The tanks continued to rumble to the south while the crews of two nearby Matildas enjoying a brew, dismissed reports of them as Antipodean exaggeration – Italian tanks simply did not do that sort of thing. Finally, they were knocked out by the anti-tank platoon of three 2-pdrs. mounted portee on trucks, Corporal A. A. Pickett accounting for four of them.

Meanwhile, the columns of prisoners streaming to the rear gave the lie to the estimated strength of the garrison. By midday, 6,000 had already reached the provosts at the collection point near Post 45 escorted by increasingly fewer guards whom the rifle companies could ill afford to detach. The defenders' morale was further shattered by a visit from three battleships, *Barham*, *Valiant* and *Warspite*, accompanied by four destroyers firing a 45-minute 15in. (380mm) programme at selected targets in the town

The second phase was now due to start and 2/5th Bn with two companies from 2/7th Bn, having covered 15 miles (24km) in nine hours, was now moving forward to take the lead on the right toward the Switch Line, but without the Matildas due to support it which had to refuel and rearm. When they advanced they came under heavy fire from enemy guns firing over open sights and supported by machine-guns, and soon the lead company was pinned down. While the battalion mortars, and Vickers machine-guns of 1 NF returned the fire, another company worked along the Wadi Scemmas, eventually collecting another 3,000 prisoners.

After Post 24 had been taken, two Matildas arrived and they helped take Post 22. Here an unfortunate incident occurred. As the prisoners were being rounded up, one shot the company commander dead, then threw down his rifle and climbed out of the pit smiling broadly. He was immediately thrown back and a Bren gun emptied into him. The company second-in-command then had to prevent his mates bayoneting the other prisoners. The incident was witnessed by the Italians at Post 25 some 500 yards (455m) away who promptly surrendered and by 1500hrs, 2/5th Bn had reached Post 20 – now less its tank support: one had left to refuel, and the other had shed a track. Another tank commander later

The Cruiser Tank Mark II and Mark IIA (A10) was originally designed as the infantry support version of the A9. But by the time its design was completed, work had begun on the Matilda, and it was reclassified as a heavy cruiser despite having a top speed of only 16mph (26km/h). Armed with a 2-pdr. gun and 1in. (30mm) of armour, the 175 built then served as a stopgap pending the arrival of the A13 and it was withdrawn from service in mid-1941. (TM – 1637/E4)

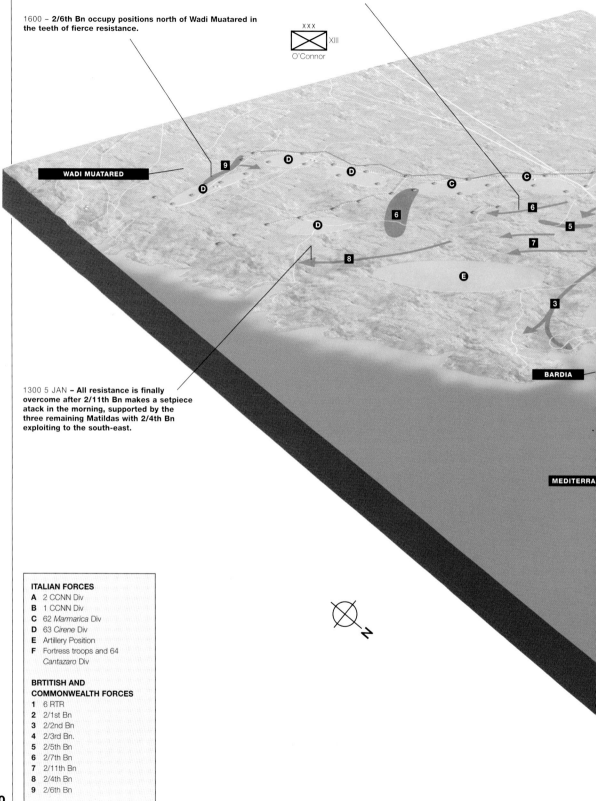

1200 – The second phase commences with 2/5th Bn from 17 Aus Bde reinforced from 2/7th Bn cross the wir [cut off] to form up on the right of 2/2nd Bn and continue towards the Switch Line, reaching Post 20 by 1500[cut off]

1600 – 2/6th Bn occupy positions north of Wadi Muatared in the teeth of fierce resistance.

X X X
XIII
O'Connor

WADI MUATARED

BARDIA

MEDITERRA

1300 5 JAN – All resistance is finally overcome after 2/11th Bn makes a setpiece atack in the morning, supported by the three remaining Matildas with 2/4th Bn exploiting to the south-east.

N

ITALIAN FORCES
A 2 CCNN Div
B 1 CCNN Div
C 62 *Marmarica* Div
D 63 *Cirene* Div
E Artillery Position
F Fortress troops and 64
   Cantazaro Div

**BRTITISH AND
COMMONWEALTH FORCES**
1 6 RTR
2 2/1st Bn
3 2/2nd Bn
4 2/3rd Bn.
5 2/5th Bn
6 2/7th Bn
7 2/11th Bn
8 2/4th Bn
9 2/6th Bn

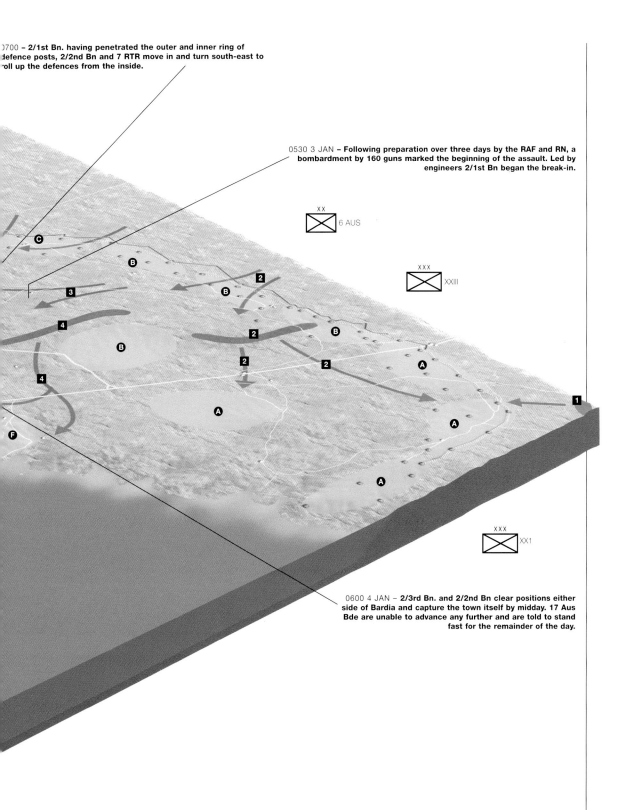

0700 – **2/1st Bn. having penetrated the outer and inner ring of defence posts, 2/2nd Bn and 7 RTR move in and turn south-east to roll up the defences from the inside.**

0530 3 JAN – **Following preparation over three days by the RAF and RN, a bombardment by 160 guns marked the beginning of the assault. Led by engineers 2/1st Bn began the break-in.**

XX
6 AUS

XXX
XXIII

XXX
XX1

0600 4 JAN – **2/3rd Bn. and 2/2nd Bn clear positions either side of Bardia and capture the town itself by midday. 17 Aus Bde are unable to advance any further and are told to stand fast for the remainder of the day.**

ASSAULT ON BARDIA 3 – 5 JAN 1941

6 Aus Div break-in viewed from the south

The flat, featureless nature of the desert landscape gave endless difficulty for the accurate artillery fire control, so any elevation was used as this Forward Observation Officer is demonstrating on his Morris Cs8. The British used a wide variety of light vehicles from various manufacturers including Morris, Commer, Bedford and Ford, many of which were Canadian built. (IWM – E1506)

described the state of his vehicle: 'Anything breakable, radio aerials, water cans, lights etc. had vanished, and evidence of no less than 46 direct hits, which says a lot for the Matilda.'

The plan had been complicated and could have broken down, but thanks to the determination of the Diggers as the fight wore on into the evening and night, they continued to progress until they had secured 3,000 yards (2,700m) of the perimeter and half the Switch Line. As we have seen, Mackay had originally wanted 2/6th Bn to mount a demonstration but the orders given by the CO, Lieutenant-Colonel A. H. L. Godfrey, began: '2/6th Battalion will capture the enemy positions on the Wadi Muatered from Post 3 to Post 11.' It was to prove a long day in the face of the most determined Italian resistance, centred on Post 11. The Aussies managed to get inside once but were thrown out and had to content themselves with surrounding it. Three times the Italians mounted fierce counter-attacks, and by the day's end, 2/6th Bn had occupied 600 yards (546 m) of the north bank of the wadi, and captured Post 7, along with part of Post 9, for the loss of 38 killed or missing and 26 wounded.

Mackay was concerned with progress. While the two brigades consolidated through the night, O'Connor, showing the sense of timing which marks great commanders, appeared by his side to discuss the matter, and agreed plans to introduce 19 Aus Bde to clear the main Italian artillery force to the south of the town. At first light, 16 Aus Bde continued to advance to either side of the town itself, whose garrison now surrendered. One Digger was seen herding prisoners, armed only with an unsheathed bayonet, with which he flicked the tops of camel-thorn. 'Everything okay Aussie?' he was asked. The Australian spat. 'I joined the army', he drawled, 'because I was tired of my old job and wanted a change, but here I am bloody droving again.'

Between midday and dusk, an estimated 10,000 prisoners were taken on a 6 mile (9km) front. To the north, a demonstration by 6 RTR and the Free French was a failure. Sergeant Harry Kirkham 'found our allies reluctant to attack. I looked behind at the FF infantry and there was not a man in sight'. However, an RTR officer, captured when his tank broke down, appeared at 2/1st Bn's HQ to report that he had talked the Italians in the coastal wadis to the north into surrendering. When told to bring them in he said 'but there are 1,500 at least'. Unable to deal with any more prisoners, the CO sent him back to hold them until the following morning.

Further south, the exhausted 17 Aus Bde found progress difficult in the face of concentrated artillery fire and, being without armour support, they were ordered to stand fast while 19 Aus Bde was brought forward to make a set-piece attack on 5 January with tanks and artillery. This plan went smoothly with 2/11th Bn attacking supported by six Matildas and 2/4th Bn passing through and exploiting. The brigade suffered only three casualties and by 1300hrs it was all over. Among the thousands of prisoners collected by 19 Aus Bde were two divisional commanders, and the Aussies were as astonished as the men of 4 Ind Div had been by the luxuries they found everywhere; enamelled baths, silk garments and cosmetics, embossed notepaper and engraved glass.

The appearance of tanks finally convinced the commander of Post 11 that honour was satisfied and he hoisted the white flag. Lt-Col Godfrey hurried forward to shake his hand while out of the post, normally garrisoned by a platoon, poured 350 Italians including 26 officers who

The capture of Sidi Barrani realised the initial objective of Operation Compass. To commemorate their arrival, the Italians had built this memorial (from a mould so they could produce many more). Now some of the thousands of prisoners make their way past it on the long march to the cages in Egypt. Transport shortages meant that most had a lot of walking to do, but in the desert there was nowhere else for them to go, so few guards were needed. (AWM – 004423)

were armed with two field and six anti-tank guns, 12 medium and 27 light machine-guns. Their resolution was one of few such instances shown by the defenders.

To their relief, the engineers found no damage to any wells or pumps and estimated an output of 400 tons per day which was handed over to 5 NZ Field Park Company. Approximately 38,300 prisoners were in the bag, together with 26 coast defence guns, 7 medium guns, 216 field guns, 26 heavy anti-aircraft guns, 41 infantry guns (65mm calibre), 146 anti-tank guns, 12 serviceable medium tanks and 115 of the useless L3s; and most important of all, 708 motor vehicles. Paraphrasing his Prime Minister, Anthony Eden declared 'never has so much been surrendered by so many to so few'. Australian losses totalled 130 dead and 326 wounded out of a Commonwealth total of 500.

Tobruk

On 5 January, Wavell instructed the Joint Planning Staff to consider a move on Benghazi as 'a matter of urgency'. The next day, Churchill demanded that another four or five squadrons of aircraft should be moved to Greece (Longmore sent two) as well as diverting reinforcements bound for Alexandria, and he confirmed Wavell's worst fears four days later by telling him he must conform his plans to 'larger interests'. Following the capture of Tobruk, all operations in Libya were to be 'subordinated to aiding Greece' which required 'prompt and active compliance'. Since well before Christmas, the Prime Minister's attention had been directed towards south-east Europe and the possibility of opening a front there and, despite O'Connor's success, this remained his priority.

During the battle of Bardia, Blenheim squadrons bombed the airfields at Gazala, Derna and Tmimi with Hurricanes patrolling to the west and Gladiators of No. 3 Sqn., RAAF providing protection to the Lysander army co-operation aircraft. So effective were these measures that the Italians failed to make any sort of appearance in the skies until the afternoon of 5 January, when the issue had already been decided. On the same day, 7 Armd Bde moved to occupy the airfield at El Adem 8 miles (13km) south of Tobruk, and the following day patrolled beyond it to the west while 4 Armd Bde moved up to Belhamed east of the port.

ABOVE **The leaping kangaroos on the side of the M13 (left) and M11 (right) on Tobruk waterfront show that they belong to 6 Cav who re-equipped following Bardia. Unlike British regiments who lettered their squadrons, the Aussies called theirs** *Ringo*, *Rabbit* **and** *Wombat*. *Ringo* **had one M11 and five M13s, and the other squadrons had two M13s each. (AWM – 005045)**

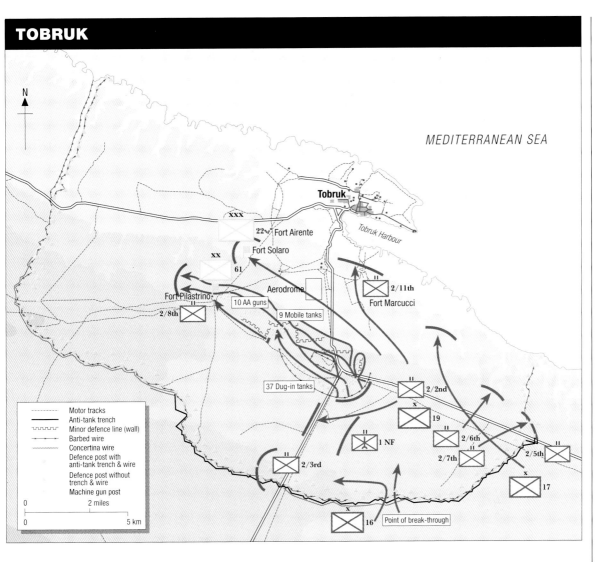

N

MEDITERRANEAN SEA

Tobruk

Tobruk Harbour

XXX

22 Fort Airente

Fort Solaro

XX

61

2/11th

Fort Pilastrino

Aerodrome

Fort Marcucci

10 AA guns

2/8th

9 Mobile tanks

37 Dug-in tanks

2/2nd

19

1 NF

2/6th

2/5th

2/7th

2/3rd

17

16

Point of break-through

Motor tracks
Anti-tank trench
Minor defence line (wall)
Barbed wire
Concertina wire
Defence post with
anti-tank trench & wire
Defence post without
trench & wire
Machine gun post

0   2 miles
0   5 km

Bir el Gubi airfield was found abandoned by 1 H and both provided testament to the success of air operations, being littered with knocked-out and broken-down aircraft. But Longmore also faced severe difficulties. He had already sent precious squadrons to Greece and his reserves were all but used up.

The latest decrypts convinced the Cabinet Defence Committee in London that a German invasion of Greece was imminent and Wavell and Longmore were ordered to Athens to consult with the Greek Prime Minister in the second week of January. While querying these instructions, and the reality of this threat, Wavell instructed O'Connor to consider raiding as far as Benghazi once Tobruk was taken, something which O'Connor already intended. The British were short of everything, and securing the harbour at Tobruk, which was significantly larger than that of Bardia, would allow most requirements to be brought in by sea. The Greeks rejected the proposed British aid as being both inadequate and provocative to the Germans assembled in Bulgaria, and consequently on 21 January, Churchill informed Wavell that Benghazi was now of the highest importance.

The M35 2in. (47mm) cannone da 47/32 anti-tank gun was a reasonable weapon for its time, capable of penetrating 17in. (43mm) of armour at 547 yards (500m). It was also used as a close support weapon. Built under licence from Boehler of Austria, each infantry division would normally have a company of 12. There were 127 such pieces among the Italian grand total including reserves, of over 1,800 guns in Libya on 10 June. (TM – 2972/A5)

Wavell decided it was necessary to simplify the chain of command. O'Connor had received instructions from Wilson's headquarters that no advance towards Benghazi was to be considered. Also, Wilson's staff was assisting with XIII Corps line of communications which, although it relieved some problems, created others. Sometimes, the wrong supplies were coming from the rear depots and O'Connor insisted that only he should control priorities. Wavell therefore decreed that XIII Corps should work direct to GHQ missing out Wilson altogether. O'Connor later commented that the following period was 'the most effective and happiest time of my command'.

On 6 January, 19 Aus Bde with two artillery regiments and 1 NF moved up to 4 Armd Bde's position and by midday on 7 January, they had deployed opposite the eastern face of Tobruk's defences, coming under sharp artillery fire. A Rifle Brigade officer described his first sight of the town: 'The view was terrific. It looked just like a scene from the Arabian Nights, the town set up on a rocky peninsula, with a touch of Arab design about it, with a sheltered harbour which could take large

Morris CS9/LAC armoured car of 11 H at Bir Sheferzen, July 1940. Armed with a Boys anti-tank rifle and a Bren gun, the Morris was built on a commercial 15cwt chassis and had only $\frac{1}{4}$in. (7mm) of armour. The spacious interior made it suitable as a command vehicle enabling a fold-down map table to be set up as shown. The parasol came from Gruppi's restaurant in Cairo and was doubtless acquired on the premise that any fool can be uncomfortable. (TM – 3470/F5)

An aerial view of Tobruk taken shortly after its capture with the fires from the *San Giorgio* and the oil terminal still burning. With an average track mileage of 1,200 on its Matildas, 7 RTR were unfit for further operations and were withdrawn by sea and rail for extensive refitting. Sir Basil Liddell-Hart said of them that 'the history of war shows no case of a single fighting unit having such a great effect in deciding the issue of battles'. (AWM – 106640)

ships.' Once more, two concentric rings of underground concrete posts were fronted by a barbed-wire entanglement and anti-tank ditch, but the latter was incomplete. The perimeter was some 30 miles (48km) in length and, according to documents captured in Bardia, the garrison manning its 128 posts commanded by Generale Petassi Manella of XXII Corps, comprised around 25,000 men, including 61 *Sirte* Div, two extra battalions, 7,000 garrison and depot troops, and demoralised stragglers from Bardia, 220 guns, 45 light and 20 medium tanks.

Thus the perimeter was longer, and the garrison smaller, than at Bardia. But the attack could not be launched immediately since it would take time to bring up sufficient ammunition and O'Connor could not risk the dwindling armour from 7 Armd Div on the fixed defences; it would once more be a task for the few remaining Matildas. The Support Group was deployed to the north with 7 Armd Bde on its left and 4 Armd Bde protecting the left flank of the Aussies. As 6 Aus Div drew up to its new objective, prisoners were brought in constantly, the remaining stragglers of Bardia heading for the supposed refuge of Tobruk bringing tales of woe and of the invincibility of the terrible Matildas. Among the 7,000 or so Italians who managed to slip away from Bardia through the rough and difficult terrain to the north was 'Electric Whiskers' Bergonzoli, and he took control of the defence.

Many Aussies took to wearing Italian boots, their own having worn out, and Italian groundsheets were also prized as they continued to live in rocky scrapes in the ground. 'Desert sores' were commonplace and fleas and lice began to add to the discomfort. On the night of 9–10 January, 16 Aus Bde moved into the line on the left of 19 Aus Bde and both proceeded with the same intense patrolling that had preceded the assault on Bardia. The patrols soon revealed a new hazard, as booby traps operated by trip wires caused casualties. In due course, it was decided that the point of break-in would be between Posts 55 and

Combat service support is unglamorous but absolutely
essential. Transport and supply was the task of the
Royal Army Service Corps, thus every other unit relied upon
them for transporting food, ammunition, fuel and water.
Water supply and route maintenance were among the
myriad responsibilities of the Corps of Royal Engineers,
while the provision and maintenance of vehicles (except
RASC) and all equipment was the responsibility of the
Royal Army Ordnance Corps.

Vickers Light Tanks were designed for reconnaissance and were precious little use for anything else. With maximum armour of just 14mm and armed with only .303 and .5in. Vickers machine-guns, it was able to cause the Italians some trouble by relying on its top speed of 35mph. However it was impotent against even the M11, and regiments equipped with it could only operate effectively by swapping squadrons with their Cruiser-equipped counterparts. (IWM – E445)

57, where the anti-tank ditch was particularly shallow, and on the night of 15–16 January, the area and its defences were carefully surveyed by two engineer officers.

O'Connor was keen to advance with 7 Armd Div to Mechili but it soon became apparent that fuel would not be available for such a move until 20 January and he agreed with Mackay to postpone this move until after the capture of Tobruk, in which 7 Armd Div would provide support. Any further advance to the west was now entirely down to the ability of the corps to keep its vehicles moving and bring forward supplies. Spare parts for all vehicles were in such short supply that any which broke down were soon cannibalised for parts and stripped within hours. This did not please the staffs, but was an indication of the pressure on the drivers. The corps plan therefore required 7 Armd Div to provide the screen to the west and south while 6 Aus Div broke in to the south-east

and fanned out through the position, thus preserving the armour for exploitation

The salient features of Mackay's plan resembled that of Bardia, with a battalion breaking in to permit the entry of the tanks of 7 RTR. He wanted to 'bite deeply into the defences and get at the enemy artillery early'. A postponement was agreed to allow as many Matildas as possible to be ready and the attack was set for 21 January. Within 7 Armd Div, only 69 cruisers and 126 Light tanks were running, and 8 H and 6 RTR handed their remaining 'runners' over to 3 and 7 H, and 1 and 2 RTR respectively then returned to Alexandria on 16 January, so that each armoured brigade now had only two regiments apiece. The passage forward of the Matildas was especially difficult as they had to be hauled up the escarpment first, for which heavy artillery tractors provided assistance to save the engines from further wear. Even then, only 18 would be available for the attack.

On 18 January, a patrol carefully marked the start line and its approaches with flannelette tied to camel-thorn bushes. For two nights previously, Wellington and Blenheim bombers dropped a total of 20 tons, while *Terror* and her supporting gunboats added to the defenders' discomfort. Then on the night 20–21 January, the Aussies advanced once more in the darkness to their forming-up positions and awaited the bombardment. The guns opened fire at 0540hrs and soon afterwards the 2/3rd Bn. advanced, led by engineers from 2/1st Fd Coy RAE with bangalore torpedoes to blow the wire. One platoon suffered 20 casualties from a booby-trap, the men 'peeling back like a

Lying badly damaged in Tobruk harbour after being bombed by the RAF some weeks before, the cruiser *San Giorgio* was able to give some useful fire support to the defenders while the Australians attacked. She was then set on fire and beached in the harbour which she shared with two scuttled merchantmen and a submarine.
(AWM – PO2038.092)

LEFT 2/1st Field Regiment, Royal Australian Artillery, in action outside Bardia. At the outset of war, Australia decided to form a second Australian Imperial Force for service overseas, and opted to number its divisions consecutively to the AIF of the First World War. As the battle honours of the original AIF were now held by the Militia, the new units were prefixed with 2/ to distinguish them from their predecessors. (AWM – 044247)

The 25-pdr. Mk II was the standard field gun of the British and Commonwealth forces. The Mark I was a development of the 18-pdr. mounted on the same carriage. The Mark II was designed in 1936 when the Royal Regiment of Artillery asked for an increase in range producing a maximum of 13,500 yards (12,285m). It was an outstanding weapon. An infantry division normally had three regiments of 24 guns, divided into two batteries of 12 at this stage of the war. (IWM – E1515)

flower opening'. There was some confusion when the bangalores were exploded, a high-spirited subaltern urged his men forward in true Aussie style. 'Go on you bastards!' he shouted and began to climb out of the ditch, before being recalled by his company commander. The battalion commander also urged them forward until the company commander explained that one of the bangalores had failed to blow. The engineers went forward to check the gaps and then the men ran towards them.

One of the lessons learned at Bardia had been the need for speed and this time, the men wore only leather jerkins over their tunics and carried only weapons, ammunition and a filled haversack. So quickly did they move that they surprised both the defenders and their neighbours. Post 56 was swiftly overrun and Posts 54 and 55 attacked, although it took half an hour to subdue Post 55. By 0645, 2/3rd Bn. had taken five posts and the lead tanks began to move forward at a steady 2.5 mph (4 km/h). By 0900hrs, they had taken Post 81; 21 posts had fallen in two and a half hours. The 2/2nd Bn were the second unit through the wire, having a similar difficult role to that of the 2/5th at Bardia. Although the weather was perfect this morning, a thick fog of dust had been whipped up, and the tanks and infantry became separated. They marched through this fog, encountering only light resistance, and reached their objectives at 0910hrs.

2/6th Bn were next through, moving to 2/2nd's right and followed by 1 NF and A Sqn, 6 Cav, equipped with a dozen captured Italian medium tanks, brightly painted with leaping kangaroos to prevent confusion. 2/6th were held up by Post 62, which was defeated by pouring a crude oil/kerosene mix into it and setting this alight. As 16 Aus Bde was fanned out, 19 Aus Bde marched deep into the Italian positions. It crossed its start line within the perimeter at 0840hrs with the infantry keeping tight up against a creeping barrage moving at 200 yards (182m) every two minutes. On the right, 2/11th Bn reached its objective without suffering a casualty, but 2/8th Bn on the left took much heavier fire after

2/4th Bn had captured the sector headquarters some 1,000 yards (910m) beyond the main road. A troop of 6 Cav with carriers and one tank was leading 2/8th Bn when they came under fierce fire. It soon became apparent that this came from ten stationary tanks that had been dug in.

A series of small actions now ensued between the infantry, armed only with small-arms, anti-tank rifles and grenades, and these immobilised pillboxes. More tanks were discovered, supported by artillery and strongpoints. Undeterred, the Aussies set to with a will and unsupported, 2/8th Bn took on a total of 22 tanks and captured over 1,000 prisoners until their momentum was exhausted. But not lost for long. The second phase was put in hand with 2/4th Bn moving towards Fort Solaro, the presumed Italian Headquarters, and 2/11th Bn sent to seize the escarpment overlooking the harbour from the south while 2/8th Bn continued towards Fort Pilastrino.

This phase began at 1400hrs with renewed artillery support from two regiments. A group of wandering Italian tanks were driven off and a fight with some anti-aircraft guns occurred at the aerodrome, but Fort Solaro proved no more than a huddle of buildings and no headquarters was found. Instead, a group of caves further west yielded what they were looking for. An Italian officer said that 'the commander' would only surrender to an officer. Lieutenant J. S. Copland went forward and accepted the surrender of the corps commander Generale Manella who handed over his pistol with tears in his eyes. 'C'est la guerre,' said Copland by way of condolence. 'Oui, c'est la guerre.' Manella replied. 'An old man, dignified, quiet and very tired.'

The 2/3rd Bn had continued to battle along the perimeter against determined opposition, but with reorganised artillery and tank support,

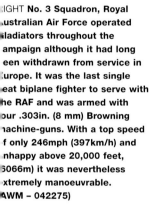

RIGHT **No. 3 Squadron, Royal Australian Air Force operated Gladiators throughout the campaign although it had long been withdrawn from service in Europe. It was the last single seat biplane fighter to serve with the RAF and was armed with four .303in. (8 mm) Browning machine-guns. With a top speed of only 246mph (397km/h) and unhappy above 20,000 feet, (6066m) it was nevertheless extremely manoeuvrable. (AWM – 042275)**

Not all of the artillery belonged to the 20th century. This ancient muzzle-loader might have been placed as a decoy to draw fire from more realistic targets; but the sangar has been carefully constructed with sufficient room for the gunners to serve the weapon, and the ramming stave suggests it was actually meant to contribute to the defence. That said, the empty Cinzano bottles indicate the detachment's faith in its abilities. (TM – 2257/B4)

ABOVE **Generale Annibale Bergonzoli, commanding the garrison at Bardia, received the following message personally from Mussolini: 'I have given you a difficult task, but one suited to your courage and experience as an old and intrepid soldier; the task of defending the fortress of Bardia to the last. I am certain that "Electric Beard" and his brave soldiers will stand, at whatever cost, faithful to the last.' Bergonzoli replied: 'In Bardia we are and here we stay.' (TM – 3454/C5)**

had reached Posts 39 and 36 by 1500hrs and proceeded to Post 34. To most of the men in the lead companies, it seemed the battle was almost over with the Italian guns largely silenced, while at Bardia they had still been firing vigorously towards the end of the first day. Once again thousands of prisoners had been taken and later that night when the lines of battle were still, some Italian bombers – in a belated response – dropped their loads on some fires, unfortunately causing appalling casualties amongst huddled groups of their comrades.

That same night, Mackay gave orders to deliver the final blow the next morning. 7 Armd Div were breaking in from the west, after making demonstrations the previous day, and 16 Aus Bde moved northwestwards towards them, while 2/4th Bn and a troop of Matildas entered the town at 1020hrs. All organised resistance had ceased by noon. The Italian Naval Headquarters and some 1,500 personnel surrendered, and a digger's slouch hat was run up the flagpole outside. Over the town lay the pall from fires of oil storage tanks and the *San Giorgio*.

Among the booty were 208 field and medium guns, 23 medium tanks and over 200 vehicles, along with wells and water distilleries sufficient to produce 40,000 gallons a day, and thousands of cases of mineral water. The garrison had enough tinned food – vegetables, fruit and veal – for two months. More than 25,000 prisoners were taken (although 'Electric Whiskers' Bergonzoli was not among them, having once more managed to slip away). Not until March was the Tobruk cage emptied. The field ambulances had to treat 306 wounded Australians (49 were killed or died of wounds) and hundreds of Italians. They were manned by some excellent surgeons, including a Jacksonian prizeman, and several Italian-speaking orderlies who proved a great help. Once again, the Australian had proved admirably suited to the unorthodox nature of the situation. The only consolation for the Italians was that now events were moving too quickly for 7 RTR and their slow Matildas. They bowed gracefully out of the campaign upon which they had so decisive an effect, for a thoroughly deserved refit.

Derna

On 22 January, O'Connor learnt from Wavell that Benghazi was now considered of the greatest importance. The Chiefs of Staff in London now proposed that it should be converted into a strong air and naval base which could be supplied by sea, rather than the difficult land route. It was these plans that prompted the immediate release westward of 7 Armd Div with 6 Aus Div directed towards Derna the following day. Ahead lay the remains of Tenth Army whose headquarters were believed to be at Cyrene, with XX Corps at Giovanni Berta, but the only complete fighting formation left was 60th (*Sabratha*) Division, together with the *Babini* Armoured Brigade and elements of other formations brought from Tripolitania. Advancing along the main metalled road, 7 Armd Bde found it blocked near Maturba. The following day, patrols had made contact with the Italians at Siret el Chreiba some 10 miles (16km) from Derna, and 4th Armd.Bde. was around 25 miles (40km) east of Mechili, with patrols to the west blocking the tracks approaching it from the west, south and south-east.

On 24 January, 4 Armd Bde engaged a force including 50 medium tanks on the Derna-Mechili track, destroying nine for the loss of one cruiser and six lights. The advance guard of 6 Aus Div drew up to Maturba at 1600hrs and relieved the British at daybreak. The carriers of A Sqn, 6 Cav probed the aerodrome under sporadic fire and although it was not heavy, it became clear that infantry action was required to clear the area. At 1230hrs 2/11th Bn dismounted from its trucks a mile from Siret el Chreiba, and the West Australians advanced astride the road. The left-hand company was engaged by two motorcycle mounted

ABOVE **In every gully, abandoned transport of every description was found. The Commonwealth forces were so short of transport that every serviceable vehicle captured was pressed into service. Finding drivers was difficult and some units used Italians – a practice that was frowned upon and eventually forbidden. Nonetheless, transport columns became more and more like gypsy caravans. (AWM – 004926)**

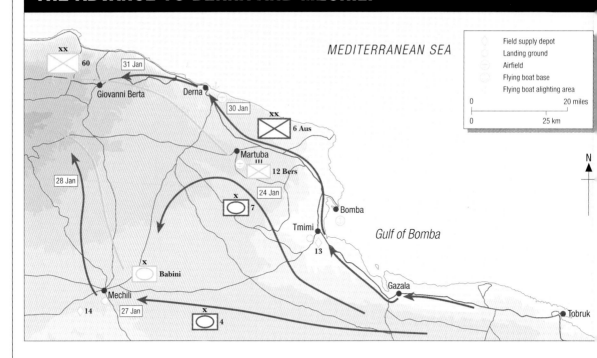

machine-guns which were quickly overrun and they moved across the open ground until machine-gun and artillery fire from ridges 2 miles (3km) away became too heavy and they went to ground. Slowly they worked their way forward, identifying four tanks and eight trucks mounting machine-guns. They were held up until the fading light enabled them to advance, securing the hangars and other airfield buildings. Meanwhile, the right-hand company had reached the north-east of the airfield overlooking Derna and the coast.

Between dawn and 0800hrs, 2/11th Bn, supported now by their own artillery, captured the ridges. The remainder of the brigade now caught them up, and a small detachment from 2/4th Bn had crossed the immense Wadi Derna to the south; up to 700 feet (213m) deep by a mile wide and considered impassable by the Italians. However, it seemed to O'Connor's headquarters that the main Italian positions were at Mechili, and he sent a message to Creagh that it was essential to prevent the Italians there escaping north-west towards Slonta. The prospects of isolating the enemy's main force seemed bright, with the Support Group blocking movement to the east and north, 4 Armd Bde to the south-west and north-west with 11 H patrolling 30 miles (48km) south of Mechili. On 26 January, 7 Armd Bde, held up previously stalled by a shortage of fuel, was ordered to cut the Mechili-Slonta track. O'Connor instructed Creagh to use the Support Group for this task if the going was too hard for tanks and also ordered Mackay to bring forward his 17 Aus Bde to attack the enemy at Mechili while 7 Armd Div contained him. The trap appeared well set.

The morning brought disappointment however. Air recce revealed that the main body of the enemy was moving north-west towards El Faidia. O'Connor was incensed that, once more, the armoured

As more and more Italian landing strips were overrun, so more and more wrecked and unserviceable aircraft were captured, together with stores and equipment. Some 1,200 aircraft were destroyed or captured on the ground as reinforcements, fed in by the Regia Aeronautica but inoperable for want of parts and maintenance had to be abandoned in a hurry. (AWM – 006494)

division had allowed the enemy to slip through its fingers due to its inefficiency at night operations, and he wrote an admonitory note. Creagh was naturally very disappointed too, and explained that bad maps, bad going and fuel shortages contributed to the failure. O'Connor remained unconvinced and replied that 'if the Italians were able to move their tanks away at night, I see no reason why we should not have been able to operate ours'. Although he was not one to dwell on such lapses, he went on to say that 'in this connection you say that the Armoured Division will be "played out" after Mechili. I'm afraid I can't agree. They will only be "played out" when there are no more tanks that can move. It is no good failing in the object of our campaign with a reserve of tanks in hand.' The armoured division had now been reduced to 50 cruisers and 95 lights and O'Connor was determined to continue, his object no less than the total destruction of Tenth Army.

An attempt by 4 Armd Bde to make amends for their failure to block the enemy was thwarted by heavy rains that turned the defiles to mud. The pursuit was called off on 29 January. By now, however, the Australians had better news to report from the north, and with the desert route open, and two fresh regiments from 2nd Armoured Division due to arrive on 7 and 9 February, O'Connor decided that the Australians could continue to exert pressure along the coast. Hopefully this would persuade the enemy that this was the main effort, and once the fresh armour and extra supplies had been brought up (which was not expected to be before 12 February) 7 Armd Div would make a swift move south-west to cut the road below Benghazi, and trap the remainder of the Italian forces in Cyrenaica. Two things might thwart this scheme. One was the difficulty of bringing up the necessary supplies which it seemed would take at least a fortnight. The second was the threat of having his forces drained to reinforce Greece.

Meanwhile, the Australians laboured in front of the Wadi Derna; 2/4th Bn faced a stiff attack on 27 January from over 1,000 Italians which they only held off with the assistance of machine-gunners from 1 NF. Resupply across the wadi was very difficult, and the CO ordered some trucks to be driven back and forth along the Maturba road to create a dust storm suggesting reinforcement. At the same time, a troop

ABOVE **Heading for Tobruk 70 miles (120km) away, Jerram imposed a strict half-speed restriction on the Matildas when out of contact, but they still needed help climbing the Escarpment to save wear and tear on their engines and vulnerable steering mechanisms. This one is being towed by a Scammel R100 artillery tractor. Although immensely busy, O'Connor made time to write to Jerram personally: 'It has been a wonderful show, and you are more than ever responsible for its success.' (TM – 1767/C3)**

of 6th Cav. tried to work its way around the southern end of the wadi and was ambushed, killing four NCOs, with three taken prisoner. On the heights above Derna itself, 2/11th Bn met fierce resistance although they managed to capture Fort Rudero with 290 men and five guns as well as a number of other posts.

The Italians continued to hold out on 28 January, their artillery being superbly sited and able to provide huge volumes of fire, reported as 'really heavy' when 'judged by 1918 European standards'. That evening, patrols of 11 H and 6 Cav. tightened the net to the south and Mackay ordered his infantry brigades to act vigorously to dislodge the enemy. But this was a difficult task, particularly in the south with its web of tangled hills. Shelling was very heavy on 29 January, especially in 2/11th Bn's area in the north-east, but in the early hours of the following morning fires were observed in Derna, and shortly after daylight a patrol reported the town abandoned, apart from a few Arabs loading loot onto the backs of donkeys.

To the west and south of Derna lay the Jebel Akhdar – the Green Mountains – rising to 2,500 feet (760m) and fertile enough for olives and oranges to grow. Rain turned the fields into bogs of red mud and the roads and tracks to quagmires. Many Aussies succumbed to sprained and broken ankles, and if the desert had been difficult, then the opportunities for defence offered by the Jebel meant there would be no let-up now. Mackay was equally worried by the poor road discipline of his columns and even directed one himself, the emphasis being very much on continuing westward as fast as possible – not helped by 'small unauthorised captured Fiat cars burning Australian Government petrol and driven by officers and others'. O'Connor had been suffering from a stomach complaint that he kept from all but his closest staff. It did not prevent him from driving himself as hard as the rest of his corps. The

A 6in. (150mm) 26cwt gun in action outside Tobruk. First entering service in 1915, these guns were withdrawn by late 1941 but gave good service during the early desert campaign. By this stage, dress codes had been abandoned for anything practical and comfortable. The gunner on the left is wearing a 'zift' hat which was very popular throughout the newly designated XIII Corps, and made from a knitted cap comforter. (AWM – 005632)

discomfort made it hard to sleep at times but he said later, it was during such sleepless periods that some of his best ideas came to him.

His plan to cut off the Italians south of Benghazi would require continued pressure through the mountains but would rely principally on his ability to refurbish 7 Armd Div The opening of Tobruk harbour to the navy was an essential starting point, but he paid tribute to 'the magnificent work of the Transport Companies … They never failed the troops on any occasion, and in spite of every difficulty, such as execrable going, and continual dust storms, their maintenance was kept up to a very high state of efficiency at all times.' FSD no. 12 was now operating at Tmimi, and 12 miles (19km) to the south lay FSD no. 13, FSD no. 14 would be opened south-west of Mechili as soon as possible.

It was hoped to be able to accumulate ten days supply of food and petrol, two complete refills of ammunition and a continuous supply of water from the FSDs, but it was estimated it would take 12 days to collect. The tanks all desperately needed overhauls, impossible without a return to the Abbassia workshops at Alexandria, so that routine maintenance would have to suffice. O'Connor decided to concentrate the most reliable vehicles from 7 Armd Bde in 4 Armd Bde ready to lead the advance when it began. Having completed these arrangements with Creagh, and having received information from aerial reconnaissance that several large Italian motorised convoys had been observed moving rapidly south, Brigadier Eric 'Chink' Dorman-Smith (acting as Wavell's liaison officer) returned to Cairo to apprise him of O'Connor's plans. O'Connor knew he had Wavell's permission to advance, and interpreted that as being without bounds.

When Dorman-Smith outlined the situation to Wavell with O'Connor's daring plan, 'all expression drained from Wavell's countenance. To marshal the pencils on his desk in a parody of

Beda Fomm, 6 February 1941
Lt Norman Plough of 2 RTR described how the Italians'
tactics 'were poor – purely frontal to our hull down position.
Instead of attacking with at least 50 tanks which might have
overrun us, they approached slowly in batches of 15 or 20.
It was fairly easy gunnery practice for us.' Once again, the
only really effective opposition came from the Italian
artillery.

ABOVE **Aussies in Derna. Derna marked the edge of the desert. To the west lay the more settled areas and in the largely undamaged town, gardens were filled with flowers, radishes cauliflowers and onions – the first fresh rations the Australians had seen in weeks. Complaints from O'Connor's headquarters that the Aussies had 'looted Derna' were vehemently denied by the provosts, and investigations revealed that the town had already been thoroughly looted four times. AWM – 005647/13)**

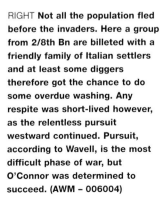

RIGHT **Not all the population fled before the invaders. Here a group from 2/8th Bn are billeted with a friendly family of Italian settlers and at least some diggers therefore got the chance to do some overdue washing. Any respite was short-lived however, as the relentless pursuit westward continued. Pursuit, according to Wavell, is the most difficult phase of war, but O'Connor was determined to succeed. (AWM – 006004)**

parade-ground drill was his form of doodling. He took them up in handfuls; they formed fours; they formed threes; they were ranked in close order and in open order. From time to time when Dorman-Smith paused for breath, he observed, "Yes Eric, I see." At the end he looked up. "Tell Dick he can go on," he said, "and wish him luck from me. He has done well."'

When Dorman-Smith returned on 2 February to O'Connor's headquarters, the Aussies were at Giovanni Berta and the opposition in front of them had simply melted away. The presence of two squadrons of 11 H operating on the Aussies' southern flank convinced the Italians that 7 Armd Div was following up behind them and they deployed no

strong flank detachment, discounting the possibility of a wide move through the desert to Msus. Graziani meanwhile had completely lost his nerve and had clearly decided to get out as fast as possible. In fact, he had decided to retreat all the way back to Tripoli 'rather than expose my person needlessly at the front' as he put it, and it was increasingly apparent to the British that the remaining Italians would soon be following him. There would be no time to await the 3,000 tons of stores, proper water supplies or even of sufficient petrol to ensure getting to the crucial position with adequate food and ammunition. There was certainly not enough time to wait for the two fresh regiments of tanks. The race to the coast was about to begin with whatever was to hand.

Beda Fomm

O'Connor faced a dilemma. He could set a trap for the Italians, but could he spring it? It would be a 150 mile (242km) march across unreconnoitred desert, with worn-out vehicles. The going was reported to be very bad indeed, and upon reaching their objective they would face a battle against a greatly superior and desperate enemy. There would be sufficient fuel to start with full fuel tanks and their own quota of food and ammunition. A convoy of lorries would follow carrying a further two days food and water and two full replenishments of ammunition. There could be no more.

They set out at dawn on 4 February with the armoured cars leading followed by 4 Armd Bde and the going proved every bit as bad as was feared. The first 50 miles (80km) were particularly so with strewn boulders and soft sand. Loose slab rock both slowed the pace and increased fuel consumption. Tellera knew from a radio intercept that Solluch was a target, but all that could be done was rush a hasty garrison to the fort there and at Sceleidima, and scatter some 'thermos bombs' along the route, further slowing the pace. However, once clear of the boulder field, a gap soon opened and 11 H disappeared in a dust cloud, clearing Msus of a few stragglers at midday. The fuel trucks had difficulty keeping up, and the increased fuel consumption was exacerbated by the damage inflicted by the flimsy fuel and water containers crashing around, many of which broke, leaking their precious fluids into the sand.

As the column closed up, dramatic news was reported from a lone Hurricane reconnaissance aircraft; it had spotted a large Italian column

As they advanced, the Commonwealth troops found more and more evidence of the effectiveness of the air campaign. Here, some curious soldiers examine a twin-engined general purpose Caproni Ca 309 *Ghibli* (Desert Wind). With the over-running of its forward bases, the Regia Aeronautica could take little further part in the campaign. Apart from its base at Benghazi, those in Tripolitania were out of range. (TM – 3407/E3)

Two abandoned L3s being examined by a despatch rider on the road overlooking Bardia from the south. The vehicle on the left appears to have been fitted with a Solothorn $^3/_4$in. (20mm) anti-tank rifle (and some rocks on the glacis plate in a desperate attempt to give it more protection). That on the right carries the more conventional twin $^1/_3$in. (8mm) Breda machine-guns. (AWM – 008413)

Beda Fomm amounted to little more than a steel-framed windmill on high ground, the only clearly visible landmark in the area. The ridges of high ground would provide some cover, enough to allow hull-down firing positions and some cover from view, but would not be an obstacle to the movement of armoured vehicles from either side. (TM – 3558/C5)

moving south from Benghazi. Although this was in actual fact a move of rear echelon units, Creagh made two decisions crucial to success, both subsequently endorsed by O'Connor. First, instead of moving west from Msus to Solluch, he moved south-west via Antelat, to the area of Beda Fomm and Sidi Saleh, to set up a blocking position in view of the certainty that the enemy was now trying to evacuate Cyrenaica completely. It was this decision that O'Connor later noted 'was mainly responsible for cutting-off the entire enemy force'. Second, having decided that the tanks needed more time for replenishment and maintenance but that speed was crucial, a fast-wheeled vanguard, Combeforce, was formed under Lt-Col Combe of 11 H, the better to reach the road quickly and cut off the retreating enemy. It comprised the armoured cars of C Sqn, 11 H, and A Sqn., 1st King's Dragoon Guards; 2nd Bn, Rifle Brigade; C Battery, 4 RHA with 25-pdr. field guns (and 160 rounds per gun) and nine 37mm Bofors anti-tank guns mounted portee on the backs of lorries from 106 (Lancashire Hussars) RHA which also operated captured 20mm Breda anti-aircraft guns.

The numbers of small arms taken were never counted, there was neither the time nor the manpower. The Italians had been in the process of converting their small arms from ¼–⅓in. (6.5–7.35mm) when the war began but had not completed the conversion. Most of the weapons were burned. In the background hospital tents from the five field hospitals set up by the Italians in anticipation of heavy casualties can be seen. (AWM – 005305)

It presented more severe logistical difficulties, for most of the necessary vehicles were a long way back in the divisional column and assembling over 140 vehicles in the correct order of march was no easy task. 4 RHA's vehicles carrying reserve ammunition had to dump it and reload with fuel and separate radio communications had to be arranged to enable the divisional command net to function. Departing shortly before sunrise on the morning of 5 February, this was the most momentous journey of the entire campaign. Through huge dust clouds visible miles away to the few remaining Italian aircraft, Combeforce struggled across the uncharted desert on compass bearings, 2,000 men in assorted vehicles with a handful of guns. At around midday they reached the road near Sidi Saleh, south of Beda Fomm. The road was empty.

With 7 Armd Div some way behind, Combe quickly established a roadblock. The action that was to follow took place in the country bordering about 15 miles (24km) of this road lying between Beda Fomm and the sea. It was sandy, but firm, and generally flat with small hummocks and a number of low ridges running from north to south. Crossed on its western side by the road was a small round hillock called The Pimple, 7 miles (11km) north of the roadblock. This gave good observation up and down the road and was later the scene of fierce fighting. To the west, stretching into the coastal sand dunes, was a large flat stretch of land.

After topping up their fuel tanks from the infantry's lorries, C Sqn, 11 H deployed into this latter area to prevent the enemy slipping past while A Sqn KDG was sent to cover the approaches from Tripolitania to the south. A Co., 2 RB dug itself in around the road with two companies

M13s attacking under shellfire. Throughout the day, units were committed piecemeal to the action. With only company commanders possessing radios, the Italian armour's inability to deploy rapidly in the British fashion severely limited objectives. Together with a lack of understanding of the principles of fire and movement, and the inherent weakness of their equipment, 2 RTR's cruisers (with those from brigade headquarters) were able to shoot them up from hull down positions again and again. (TM – 3182/D5)

and eight of the anti-tank guns deploying to the rising ground to the east. The ninth anti-tank gun was dismounted and deployed in defilade in the sandhills while the fourth rifle company with the field guns took up a position behind them, refusing the right flank. The position of 106 RHA's anti-aircraft guns is unknown, but two were certainly positioned in cover either side of the road. It was hardly an ideal position to present a delaying action, much less to block a much larger force. The infantry barely had time to dig in and lay a few mines before the first Italians arrived at about 1430hrs.

A long convoy of some 5,000 troops and civilian refugees came into sight. Immediately some trucks went up on mines or to the armoured cars and 25 pdrs. Fearful as they were of the carriers and captured Italian tanks of the Australian divisional cavalry regiment, the Italians had concentrated their strength to their rear. With most of their fighting troops still to the north, those clogging the road against Combeforce largely comprised administrative units. Taken completely by surprise, the escorting battalion of 10th Bersaglieri Regiment began a series of disconnected and uncoordinated attacks upon the roadblock. Lacking armour and artillery support, the infantry and artillery of Combeforce threw them back twice and then a third time while the armoured cars raced up and down shooting up any target that presented itself.

With pressure beginning to mount on the roadblock, Caunter's 4 Armd Bde arrived late in the afternoon. Combe suggested to Creagh that he attack the column immediately from the ridges to the east. Caunter was passing through Antelat when his signallers intercepted this message and he readily agreed, launching 3 H, 7 H and 2 RTR at the steadily lengthening column. 7 H reached Beda Fomm itself at about 1700hrs. From here, they could see the Italian column stretched out in both directions and immediately set to attack. Gathering dusk brought

the action to a close, but not before two more columns of vehicles and artillery had been shot up by the light of a burning petrol tanker.

A Hussar sergeant, armed with no more than a Very pistol, was assisted in his control of a group of prisoners by one of their number, who handed him an automatic. Speaking excellent English with an American accent, the helpful prisoner had lived in the USA for 11 years. Two M-13s were captured by Lt Norman Plough of 2 RTR who came upon them broadside when his cruiser reached the end of a line of shot-up transport, held up by a roadblock his squadron had made out of two single-decker buses. He told Trooper Eldred 'Taffy' Hughes to get the crews out, which Hughes proceeded to do by rapping on the turrets with his revolver. While marching them back, Hughes encountered 'an Eytie officer in a beautiful powder-blue uniform with gold-braid everywhere'. He was promptly ordered to 'fall in' which he did under protest. Hughes was later awarded a Distinguished Conduct Medal.

Many Italians came in and gave themselves up overnight and many more slipped through the seaward flank, where some were collected by 1 KDG in the south. The KDGs reported no serious threat other than failing radio batteries, and Combeforce generally was short of food and ammunition. The guns of 4 RHA were down to 30 rounds each and they requested urgent resupply but were told they would have to make do for now. Indeed, the British artillery was now immobile, every last drop of

A 37mm Bofors anti-tank gun carried 'portee'. Said to be the idea of a Rhodesian officer, Lt. Gillson, the portee avoided dragging the guns over the rough terrain which did them no good. Although they could be dismounted, they usually fought mounted for the benefit of mobility despite leaving the detachment horribly vulnerable. The 37mm which equipped 106 RHA was slightly less powerful than the 2-pdr. (IWM – 2300)

petrol from whatever source was directed to the armour. Even the worn out vehicles of 7 Armd Bde would be required before the action was through. The Italians were surrounded but by a perilously thin cordon. Fortunately, their persistent inability to mount proper reconnaissance meant that they did not know this. Their view was that large and powerful forces held them in a vice, deepening a belief, now long nurtured, that Rome had failed to equip them for modern warfare. Eau de Cologne and Parma ham would certainly prove of little value against bloody-minded soldiers who had just spent a miserable night in cold and wet holes in the ground.

The Aussies entered Barce on the 5th, accompanied by the detonation of a vast ammunition dump in a mushroom cloud shortly after the arrival of the lead patrols, and were bearing down on the rear of the column now 11 miles (18km) long. Tellera ordered 'Electric Whiskers' Bergonzoli to break out of the trap – truly a poisoned chalice. Artillery was arriving in quantity, but with the *Babini* Armoured Brigade dissipated to provide rear protection against the Aussies and flank protection against the Support Group, he was deprived of resources and distracted. He planned to mount a holding attack against Combeforce while swinging whatever armour he could scrape together around the Pimple, before swinging south to take the roadblock in the flank and rear. Meanwhile, Creagh ordered the Support Group (1 KRRC and a few guns) to head for Sceleidima and on to attack the rear of the column near the coast, while Combeforce and 4 Armd Bde were to maintain their grip. Their tank strength comprised two cruisers and three lights in brigade headquarters, seven cruisers and six lights with 3 H, one cruiser and 29 lights with 7 H, and 12 cruisers and seven lights with 2 RTR. Caunter believed the critical point would be at Beda Fomm, but

When the Aussies entered Benghazi recorded the Australian Official History, 'the citizens, who included many Greeks and Jews as well as Italians and Arabs [the normal population exceeded 50,000], waved and cheered'. Assisted by an English speaking Greek priest, they called the Australians 'our brave Allies'. The main column entered the next day and was received politely by the 'amiable citizens' who apparently included many Italian soldiers in civilian clothes. (AWM – 005845/26)

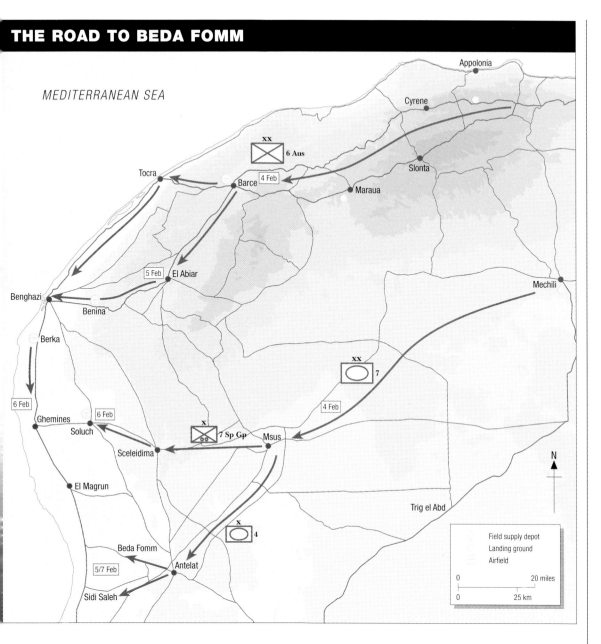

Creagh refused to commit 7 Armd Bde to him (consisting of just the ten cruisers and eight lights of 1 RTR) as it constituted his only armoured reserve. But by retaining it under 7 Armd Bde command, he also prevented Caunter, the man on the spot, from directly communicating with them and thus fully integrating them into the battle.

The following day resolved into two separate but related battles: Combeforce's roadblock at Sidi Saleh and 4 Armd Bde around Beda Fomm. Strong wind, laden with rain, greeted the combatants on the morning of 6 February, and visibility was constantly being reduced throughout the day by sudden squalls and scudding rain. As the daylight spread, it revealed the Italians strung-out in a disjointed column along miles of road. Some had made the effort to dig shell scrapes and unlimber guns, but most of them sat tight in their vehicles with the engines running, hoping they would be able to edge forwards and break out of the trap. The greater spirit and determination displayed by the Italian tankies over their previous efforts in the campaign proved of no avail.

With 3 and 7 H operating along the length of the column to the north, the first attack against 2 RTR around the Pimple began at 0830hrs. The first group of 10 M-13s were greeted by A13 cruisers from A Sqn in hull-down positions 600 yards (546m)away and swiftly knocked out. A Sqn retired onto the next ridge a mile to the east (known as 'the Mosque' because of a conspicuous white tomb), from which they knocked out another seven M-13s while C Sqn's slower A9s and A10s manoeuvred around The Pimple, accounting for another eight Italian tanks. A column that moved away towards Combeforce was chased and destroyed by A Sqn, yielding 350 prisoners.

The Pimple soon erupted under Italian artillery fire and 2 RTR sustained hits. Ammunition was also getting dangerously low. By noon some 40 of the Italian medium tanks had been knocked out or abandoned, but there still appeared to be 50 or so in action. With 7 H's sole cruiser breaking down (hurriedly repaired over 25 frightening minutes within 2,000 yards (1,800m) of the enemy) 1 RTR's support was desperately needed; but it was having communications difficulties and appeared to be lost in a sandstorm somewhere near Antelet. Trooper 'Topper' Brown of 2 RTR described the fighting that day: 'Practically all morning we never stopped firing at wagon loads of infantry or tanks … We definitely had a score of 20 M-13s at the end of the day. At times we

An A10 with two knocked-out M13s in the background. It belonged to B Sqn, 2 RTR which was attached to 3 H, although it carries C Sqn markings. The crew was captured when a track was shot away; probably the only prisoners taken by the Italians at Beda Fomm, but released the following day. (TM – 1637/E4)

were getting overwhelmed and had to keep withdrawing to the Pimple, Italian artillery knocked out four 2 RTR cruisers who ran out of ammo. At 1300hrs the RASC brought up their ammo lorries and the remaining ten cruisers were topped up with fuel and ammo.'

When 2 RTR was ready to rejoin the action at 1415hrs having lost three more tanks through breakdowns, the Pimple was occupied by Italian artillery, so they took up a position a mile to the south. Caunter sent repeated requests for the cruisers of 7 Armd Bde to join him, but faulty communications meant they had to fight on alone. By 1500hrs, although 7 H had found the tail of the column, they had encountered several M-13s which moved down into 3 H's area. They had orders not to let them pass but little means apart from bluff and manoeuvring. With the RHA's observation post temporarily out of action, a crisis had been reached. But having restored communications with their OP, and battery, they silenced the enemy artillery on the Pimple, 2 RTR were able to return at 1600hrs. With 2 RTR again running short of

LEFT **Some of the booty from the campaign was displayed in Alexandria including these Breda 20mm anti-aircraft guns, enough of which were serviceable to equip a battery of 106 RHA, the Lancashire Hussars Yeomanry. The Lancashire Hussars were Territorials from west Lancashire, one of a number of cavalry regiments that converted to artillery in the 1920s, and would help deliver the coup de grace at Beda Fomm. They were subsequently destroyed in Greece and Crete. (TM – 2833/E1)**

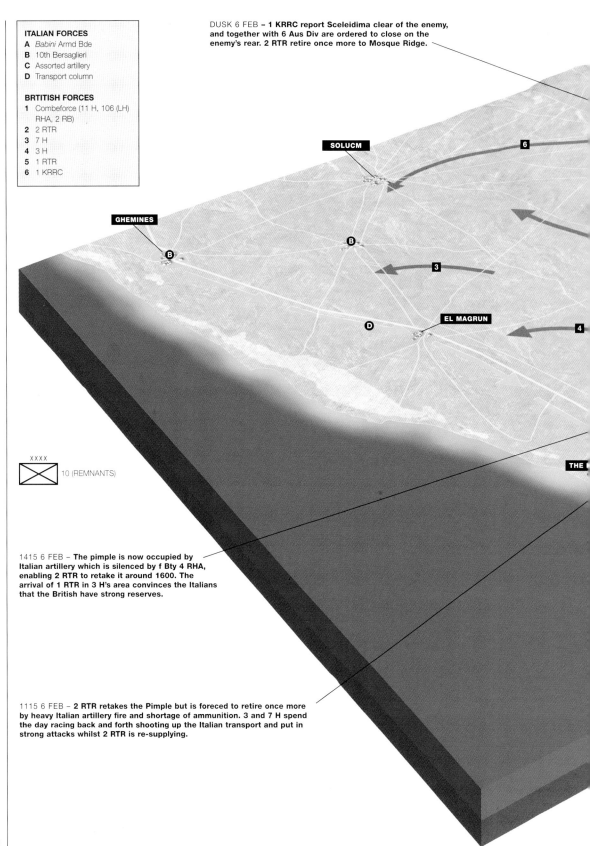

ITALIAN FORCES
A *Babini* Armd Bde
B 10th Bersaglieri
C Assorted artillery
D Transport column

BRTITISH FORCES
1 Combeforce (11 H, 106 (LH)
  RHA, 2 RB)
2 2 RTR
3 7 H
4 3 H
5 1 RTR
6 1 KRRC

DUSK 6 FEB – **1 KRRC report Sceleidima clear of the enemy,
and together with 6 Aus Div are ordered to close on the
enemy's rear. 2 RTR retire once more to Mosque Ridge.**

SOLUCM

GHEMINES

B

B

3

D

EL MAGRUN

4

THE

xxxx
10 (REMNANTS)

1415 6 FEB – **The pimple is now occupied by
Italian artillery which is silenced by f Bty 4 RHA,
enabling 2 RTR to retake it around 1600. The
arrival of 1 RTR in 3 H's area convinces the Italians
that the British have strong reserves.**

1115 6 FEB – **2 RTR retakes the Pimple but is foreced to retire once more
by heavy Italian artillery fire and shortage of ammunition. 3 and 7 H spend
the day racing back and forth shooting up the Italian transport and put in
strong attacks whilst 2 RTR is re-supplying.**

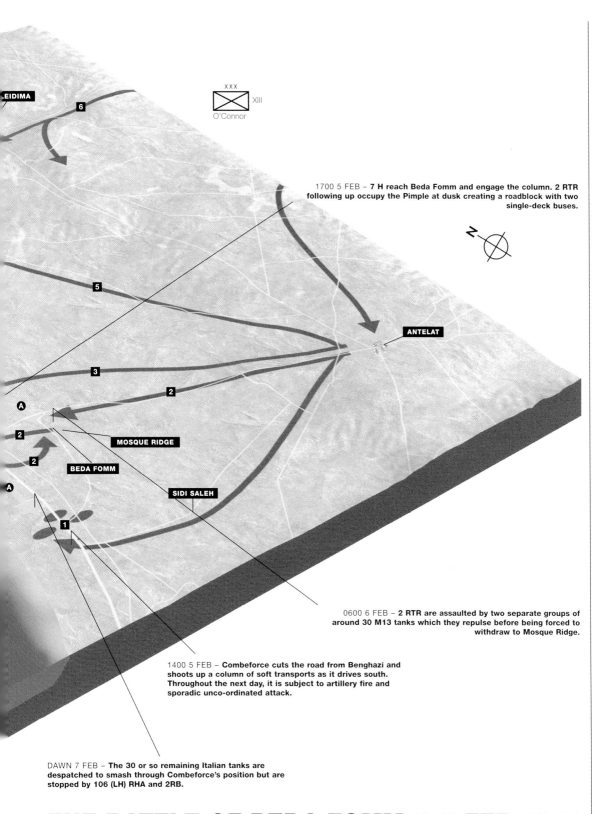

.EIDIMA

6

XXX
⊠ XIII
O'Connor

1700 5 FEB – **7 H reach Beda Fomm and engage the column. 2 RTR following up occupy the Pimple at dusk creating a roadblock with two single-deck buses.**

N

5

ANTELAT

3

2

A

2

MOSQUE RIDGE

2

BEDA FOMM

A

SIDI SALEH

1

0600 6 FEB – **2 RTR are assaulted by two separate groups of around 30 M13 tanks which they repulse before being forced to withdraw to Mosque Ridge.**

1400 5 FEB – **Combeforce cuts the road from Benghazi and shoots up a column of soft transports as it drives south. Throughout the next day, it is subject to artillery fire and sporadic unco-ordinated attack.**

DAWN 7 FEB – **The 30 or so remaining Italian tanks are despatched to smash through Combeforce's position but are stopped by 106 (LH) RHA and 2RB.**

THE BATTLE OF BEDA FOMM 5–7 FEB 1941

Combeforce cuts off the Italian retreat and holds them until supported by 7 Armd Bde

ammunition, Caunter requested that 1 RTR move down to the Pimple but continuing communications difficulties prevented this happening before nightfall. 2 RTR again withdrew for replenishment covered by a smokescreen and The Pimple changed hands once more.

Meanwhile, at the roadblock during the morning, the Italians persistently battered at the door held shut by Combeforce. Their attacks varied in strength and cohesion but all were repulsed. At about 1040hrs, three columns led by infantry and containing numerous vehicles advanced. Those following the track to the east of the road and in the dunes were soon stopped and surrendered while the one moving along the road which was supported by tanks and guns appeared ready to fight. A duel was fought between an Italian 75mm field gun and one of 106 RHA's portees at exactly one kilometre range (both guns were beside kilometre stones). No damage was sustained by the portee but the Italian detachment gave up when two 37mm holes appeared in their gun shield. An hour later, this column also surrendered.

The British positions were under constant shellfire throughout the day but the commander of 2 RB's Headquarter Company, now that there was no direct threat, decided to erect the Officers' Mess marquee several hundred yards behind the reserve company, where it attracted considerable attention from the Italian gunners. Finally, at nightfall, some 30 Italian tanks and vehicles, which broke past 2 RTR to the west at around 1800hrs, headed south towards Combeforce, arriving at 2100hrs. Some mines laid on the road had been lifted and some of the Italians managed to break right through the roadblock. Four tanks were destroyed while one anti-tank portee's crew were killed or wounded when a shell exploded in their gun shield; another four tanks and some lorries broke through, but the rest and the 500 accompanying infantry abandoned the attempt. Mines were hastily relaid and another attack yielded another 150 prisoners before a final effort was made along the seaward side of the road around midnight. This was dealt with by 106 RHA, now reinforced by two more portees which had recently arrived.

Bergonzoli realised his plan was not going to work. The total remaining tank strength left to him was about 30, and he decided to use them frontally against Combeforce. O'Connor had spent the previous day at Creagh's side and with the Support Group reporting the capture of Sceleidima he directed them to close on the rear of the column. Mackay was also told to despatch two infantry battalions in lorries for the same purpose. All through the battle, the Aussies to the north had been pushing on. Engineers slaved desperately to open the way amid the wreckage of retreat, and they rushed to reach Benghazi through the mud and rain, with the first of them entering the town among cheering crowds that evening.

It was a miserable night for the riflemen and gunners, in slit trenches huddled against the rain and cold with hardly any sleep. One platoon of 2 RB guarding 400 prisoners had to deal with two tanks that appeared around 0400hrs causing their charges to stampede. They managed to capture the tanks and calm down their prisoners. Ammunition arrived but the cordon looked very thin. At 0630hrs, following a heavy artillery concentration and having evaded 4 Armd Bde, the final desperate Italian attack was pressed home hard. The M-13s firing on the move –

against the best gunnery practice of the time – now found themselves in a duel with the anti-tank guns of 106 RHA. Trading shot for shot, the vulnerable little guns were knocked out one by one, while the infantry were held off by the riflemen until they too were overrun. In ferocious hand-to-hand fighting, the guns of C Bty, 4 RHA received permission to bring down fire on the riflemen's positions.

The commander of the anti-tank battery, Major R. S. Burton, later wrote: 'All our anti-tank guns did very well … Sergeant Gould knocked out six tanks at extremely close range – he handled [his portee] very cleverly – getting some tanks in the rear as they ran down the road past his position. He received an immediate DCM.' Meanwhile, taking control of the portee damaged the previous afternoon, Burton himself, together with his batman and a cook, drove it off to a flank, and put five rounds into five Italian tanks. The Rifle Brigade anti-tank rifles and the 25-pdrs. accounted for the rest with the last one knocked out just 20 yards (18m) from the Officers' Mess tent.

With the descent of an eerie silence, it became apparent that, with no more tanks, the Italians had no way to fight their way out of the trap. White flags began to appear here and there along the column and vehicles and equipment were abandoned in a flurry of surrenders. Lt-Col Callum Renton, commanding 2 RB, asked Burton and his men to parade before him where he personally thanked them on behalf of his battalion who had suffered only three dead and four wounded.

On hearing that it was all over, O'Connor turned to Dorman-Smith and said, 'We'd better send a message to Archie, what shall we say?' Dorman-Smith thought a hunting metaphor would appeal to Wavell. It read: 'Fox killed in the open …' The full message was sent to Cairo in clear for Mussolini's benefit. 'I think this may be termed a complete victory,' O'Connor later wrote, 'as none of the enemy escaped.' A little later, O'Connor visited the captured Italian generals and apologised for the rough conditions where they were being held. 'Thank you very much,' replied Generale Ferdinando Cona, 'we do realise you came here in a very great hurry.'

AFTERMATH

Some of the 25,000 prisoners taken at Tobruk are marched away. It was a difficult task to look after them in the aftermath of the battle, but the 2/7th and then 2/2nd Bns strove unceasingly to feed and water them, encouraging them to sing to keep up their morale and sometimes singing back. (AWM – 00595)

'Do you know what we call your general?' a senior Australian officer asked one of O'Connor's staff officers. 'The little terrier, because he never lets go.' At the Rifle Brigade's Regimental Headquarters near the knocked-out Italian tank, with a mess tent that seemed to Dorman-Smith like 'a collapsed elephant', a party was in progress. Smashed lorries, bodies, abandoned piles of equipment, guns and tanks lay in a formless jumble of litter. Over 25,000 prisoners, 216 guns, 1,500 wheeled vehicles and over 100 tanks (enough of which were serviceable to re-equip 6 RTR) were captured in this battle which cost just 25 British casualties. That brought the total haul for the campaign to an astonishing 130,000 prisoners (later put at 110,000) including 22 generals, an admiral and the official Italian Army brothel, 180 medium and 200 light tanks, innumerable soft-skin vehicles and

Among the prisoners were some 1,500 naval personnel, including their admiral, Massimiliano Vietina, whom the Aussies found standing on the steps of the naval barracks immaculately attired complete with white gloves. With his Fiat idling nearby, he smoked a cigar as his men – bags already packed – were marched off into captivity. Meanwhile, in place of the Italian flag which had flown from the tall staff nearby, an Aussie hoisted his own battered slouch hat. (AWM – 005415)

845 guns captured at a cost of 500 dead, 1,373 wounded and 55 missing. Compass said Wavell, 'could not have been executed without the magnificent support given by the Royal Air Force and Royal Navy'. Italian records show they lost 58 aircraft in combat (during the Compass period), 91 captured intact on their airfields and no less than 1,100 damaged and captured. RAF losses for the same period (all causes) were 6 Hurricanes, 5 Gladiators, 3 Wellingtons and 1 Valentia.

O'Connor was all for finishing the job and keen to proceed. He was sure he could take Tripoli and clear the Italians from North Africa altogether, despite the battered condition of his equipment and tiredness of his men. However, the success of the operation so far merely meant one less thing for Wavell to worry about. When Dorman-Smith went to see him to present O'Connor's plans in Cairo on 12 February, the maps of the desert that had dominated the long wall were replaced by those of Greece. 'You see, Eric,' said Wavell, gesturing towards it, 'I'm planning my spring campaign.' Despite achieving what appeared to Churchill as a small miracle, the order to go on the defensive were issued the same day. The day before, Wavell had received instructions from the Defence Committee to send an expeditionary force to Greece before the Germans invaded. Although this was reconsidered and confirmed with Wavell's support two weeks later, the brief opportunity had passed.

Many of the units from Cyrenaica, including 6 Aus Div, were to find themselves sent to Greece where they were in turn routed in the German invasion a few weeks later. It would be a long time before the British would get another sniff of Tripoli because on the same day they were ordered to halt, there arrived in Libya another fox – Erwin Rommel, soon to be followed by the first elements of the Deutsches Afrikakorps.

CHRONOLOGY

1940 **10 June:** Italy declares war on France and Great Britain.

11 June: The Regia Aeronautica launches the first air raid on Malta; 11 H commence operations in Libya.

21 June: Italian invasion of France.

22 June: France signs armistice with Germany.

24 June: France signs armistice with Italy.

28 June: Italian commander Maresciallo Italo Balbo is killed. Replaced by Maresciallo Rodolfo Graziani.

9 July: British and Italian battle fleets engage. Italians retire after sustaining damage.

3 August: Italians invade British Somaliland.

19 August: British evacuate Somaliland.

13 September: Italians invade Egypt, capturing Sollum.

16 September: Italians occupy Sidi Barrani.

17 September: The Luftwaffe defeated in Battle of Britain and invasion is postponed indefinitely.

28 October: Italians invade Greece.

11/12 November: Fleet Air Arm attack cripples the Italian battle fleet at Taranto.

9 December: Operation Compass begins.

10 December: Sidi Barrani recaptured.

12 December: 7 Armd Div pursuit to Buq Buq.

17 December: Sollum reoccupied.

24 December: Bardia invested.

1941 **3-5 January:** 6 Aus Div captures Bardia.

21-22 January: 6 Aus Div captures Tobruk.

28 January: Italians abandon Wadi Derna line.

5 February: 7 Armd Div establishes roadblock at Beda Fomm.

7 February: Italian Tenth Army surrenders.

12 February: Generalleutnant Erwin Rommel arrives in Tripoli.

BIBLIOGRAPHY

Operation Compass tends to be overlooked in literature in favour of later campaigns involving Rommel and the Deutsches Afrikakorps. However, it bears further study as it is not only one of the few bright spots in Britain's early war record, but as a comparison between a modern, forward looking (albeit desperately straitened) military machine and one rooted in the past. (Something of an irony when one considers the nature of British equipment at the time and their subsequent tactical inflexibility). It is however, immensely important to anybody interested in the later campaigns to understand the context (including the strategic and naval aspects as well as the military) in which they were fought, to say nothing of the interesting nature of the campaign itself.

John Baynes, *The Forgotten Victor*, (Brassey's, 1989)
> This provides a detailed biography of O'Connor, from his service in Italy during the First World War to the command of a brigade on the North-West Frontier of India which he regarded as pivotal in his own development as an officer. Following Beda Fomm, O'Connor was captured and later escaped from Italy to serve as a corps commander under Montgomery in Normandy.

BELOW **An armoured car of the KDGS passing wreckage from the Italian column just in front of The Pimple. The feature changed hands repeatedly and was a principal position for the Italian gunners who once more demonstrated tremendous valour. A fierce battle was being fought around it when the belated appearance of 7 Armd Bde, who had gamely driven towards the sound of gunfire in 3 H's sector, halted the counter-attack there and convinced the Italians that the British possessed ample reserves of armour. (TM – 2555/E6)**

Corelli Barnett, *The Desert Generals*, (William Kimber, 1960)
Regarded as something of a minor classic, Barnett's work has been extensively reprinted. It describes the action through a chronological sequence and concentrates on the performance of the British senior officers. Unfortunately, it was written before the release of information on Ultra and it naturally lacks detail on the importance of this singular intelligence source.

John Connell, *Wavell: Scholar and Soldier*, (William Collins, 1964)
Although there have been excellent biographies of Wavell published more recently, this remains the best description of Wavell's early life and career up until his relief as Commander-in-Chief by Auchinleck. (A second volume covers his later life.)

George Forty, *General O'Connor's Desert Triumph Dec 1940 – Feb 1941: The First Victory*, (Nutshell Publishing, 1990)
A superb and extensively illustrated history of the campaign that also includes much about related air and naval operations. George Forty is a former curator of the Tank Museum and has interviewed a number of the participants.

Ronald Lewin, *The Chief*, (Hutchinson, 1980)
A relatively recent and very well written appraisal of Wavell as a senior commander form his time as Commander-in-Chief Middle East to Viceroy of India. It benefits from Mr Lewin's earlier work, especially concerning Ultra. (See also his *Ultra Goes to War* [1978])

Harold E. Raugh Jr, *Wavell in the Middle East: A Study in Generalship*, (Brassey's, 1993)
The most thorough and well researched study of Wavell's time as Commander-in-Chief, written by a West Point instructor. It is well worth reading to understand the enormity of the responsibilities and the complexities of the problems facing Wavell during his difficult year in command.

Gavin Long, *Australia in the War 1939-1945: To Benghazi*, (Australian War Memorial, 1952)
The Australian Official History gives immense detail on the actions of the units and individuals of the Second Australian Imperial Force, from formation through movement to the Middle East and training as well as the operations themselves. In this respect it is the most thorough account of the campaign.

Kenneth Macksey, *Beda Fomm: The Classic Victory*, (Pan/Ballantine, 1971)
Part of an extensive series of small paperbacks published in the late sixties/early seventies, Kenneth Macksey's account is an excellent one-volume description of campaign. It is also well illustrated with maps, drawings and photos although it is quite difficult to find these days.

Bryan Perret, *Armour in Battle: Wavell's Offensive*, (Ian Allen, 1979)
Another pictorial history, mainly utilising photos from the Imperial War Museum and written by another Osprey author. It also provides extensive technical detail on equipment used by both sides.

Barrie Pitt, *The Crucible of War: Western Desert 1941*, (Jonathan Cape, 1980)
Part one of a two volume account of the Desert Campaign, this is a lucid description of the campaign but also of the preparations in

the Middle East prior to war and of the other campaigns in the region, most notably in Abyssinia.

I. S. O. Playfair (et. al.,) *History of the Second World War: The Mediterranean and the Middle East*, Vol I; (HMSO 1954)

The British Official History gives the most complete account of the war in the Mediterranean theatre, helping to set the campaign in its wider context and explaining the strategic dimension, although its scope precludes it from giving too much detail on individual unit actions.

WARGAMING THE CAMPAIGN

There are a multitude of wargaming possibilities arising from this campaign, particularly at the tactical level. The Italians were far from the cowards portrayed in the Allied press (very much a device for home consumption) and proved consistently that they did not lack individual courage. Innumerable examples are testament to their individual bravery. What they lacked was collective morale which, given the deficiencies of their military machine was hardly surprising, and was compounded by the vast gulf that existed between officers and men – something noted by both Allied and later German observers. At this stage, the British were almost all Regular and professionals and those who were not (especially the Australians) had such superb spirit as to overcome their inexperience. Therefore it should be possible to create a wide variety of tactical scenarios in which relatively small groupings face each other.

At this smaller end of the scale, skirmish games can be created involving 11 H armoured cars or 'Jock' columns versus miscellaneous Italian groupings, either holding defensive positions or moving around on the Libyan side of the wire. A simple solo game can be easily produced for a squadron group involving encounters with randomly generated Italian groupings, drawn perhaps from a deck of cards. In these desert operations, terrain will be very simple but the distances large, so it might be that games are generated on a map divided into a dozen or so squares with each one representing a table top and

Almost as soon as the firing stopped, Bedouin appeared and began to loot the column. O'Connor said he had never seen such a scene of wreckage and confusion as existed along its line. Orders were given that the looting should be stopped, which the Bedu found incomprehensible, and unfortunately one of them was shot. (3189/B2)

containing a different Italian grouping. Armoured actions could be fought between squadron groups of roving British tanks against their Italian opposite numbers in the region south and west of Tobruk, or a change of scenery might be provided by the Australians trying to push through the Jebel Akhdar. The Italians were very often brave and tenacious opponents when given a position to defend with reasonable artillery support, and this would be a good scenario for a battalion level game using *WRG, Hell by Daylight* or similar rules. The ground is likely to be much closer than in the open desert providing the Italian player with reasonable scope for defence without being reliant on supply factors and Australian player with more of a challenge than perhaps he expects.

Furthermore at this level, specific actions such as the attacks on the camps or the battle at Beda Fomm provide scenarios for either individual games. These could easily be developed into mini-campaigns by the linking of the two actions at Beda Fomm or by attempting the attacks on Bardia or Tobruk. Here, the fight can either be played following the broad historical scenario or a number of maps might be used to give the attacker different options and the defender a chance to come up with a more effective plan. However, having selected his concept of defence, the Italian player should be restricted to only local counter-attacks and the Australian's artillery support limits the point of break-in until such time as he can expand a breach. Whatever the setup, at this level of game, the problems will be largely tactical. The Italians' main problem in these circumstances will revolve around command and control. Having set their positions, it is very difficult for them to manoeuvre. The Aussies on the other hand, need to collect intelligence and plan thoroughly and in detail.

For the more adventurous players or club, there remains the campaign itself, the size of which makes it tempting. Unfortunately, it is

Although overshadowed by later events, Wavell's '30,000' had in O'Connor's masterly campaign, indeed 'risen to the heights of circumstances'. No more apt tribute has been paid than that of Corelli Barnett, who said: 'Their brilliance sparkles against the darkest setting of the war; hardly rivalled, never surpassed'. (IWM – E1380)

not well represented in the field of commercial board games being overshadowed by Rommel's later exploits. This is perhaps not so serious since despite their enormous numerical superiority, in desert operations, the badly administered and largely immobile Italian army was always at a severe handicap in the face of a fast, mobile, and well run smaller force, and it would be difficult to make up form this imbalance. However, with only a couple of divisions but varied troop types on one side and a large number of fairly homogenous divisions on the other, it is not too large to be fought using *Command Decision* or *Corps Commander* type rule sets. However, a singular feature of desert campaigns, more than others, is the importance of supply and therefore of transport. At this level, rules must account for what can be done, for although the desert is a tactician's dream, it is a logistician's nightmare.

The overwhelming problems facing higher level commanders were administrative and this must be reflected in the game. A system must be in place for daily maintenance requirements for each unit which recognises tat every ounce of food, fuel and water must be brought forward. Both sides must consider stocking dumps and be aware of the limits on manoeuvre imposed by supply. The real problem revolves around transport. The British will start with adequate transport resources, but the wastage of vehicles was enormous (around 40 per cent in the desert), and this coupled with the increasing distance from their base made up most of O'Connor's problems. If a simple and reliable means of accounting for supply is covered in the campaign rules (including vehicle wastage) then the true nature of desert warfare will become apparent in the course of playing the campaign – the balancing of risks is the key to British success.

Some players may be put off by the thought of complicated book-keeping but it really does not have to be so – a simple figure (say a ton of supplies per battalion per day) will suffice. To this must be added ammunition for the artillery and armour (which will also require a separate fuel requirement) and then a simple calculation of distance from the source gives a figure for sustainability. (Lorries will average only 20kph over long distances, will require two hours to load or unload and should be able to work no more than 16 hours per day.) Maintenance can be factored in by reducing the average speed according to the avaliability or otherwise of workshop units. These rough and ready calculations will work quite adequately to provide playable logistic restraints which are essential. Wavell said that the more he saw of modern warfare, the more it seemed to be a matter of administration. Logistics are the art of the possible, especially in the desert and as the saying goes, amateurs think tactics, professionals think logistics. If, at any stage, it has sounded as though the victory was easy, you are welcome to try and do as well yourself.

INDEX

Figures in **bold** refer to illustrations

Abyssinia 36
Aphis, HMS 32, 40, 46

Balbo, Maresciallo Italo (1896-1940) 14
Bardia 11, 13, 40, 41, **41**, 44-49, **46**, **47**, **50-51**(map), 52-53
Beda Fomm **70-71**, 73-81, **74**, **82-83**(map), 84-85
Benghazi 54, 55, 57, 65, **78**, 84
Bergonzoli, Generale Annibale (1884-1973) 14, **64**, 78, 84
Berti, Generale Mario 14, 27
Bir el Gubi 55
booby traps 57, 61-62
British and Commonwealth forces
  4th Indian Division 36
    16th British Brigade 35-36, 44
    Royal Fusiliers 33
    Selby Force 35, 36
  7th Armoured Division 22, 22-23, 44, 57, 60, 61, 64, 65, 66, 67
    4th Armoured Brigade 8, 9, 11, 34, 40, 54-55, 65, 67, 76, 79
      7th Queen's Own Hussars 9, 34, 35
    7th Armoured Brigade 11, 37, 39, 54, 79
    11th Hussars 8, 8-9, 11, 12, 34, 72
    Support Group 11
      King's Royal Rifle Corps 8
  6th Australian Division **42-43**, 65, 88
    16th Australian Brigade 44, 45, 52, 57, 62, 64
    17th Australian Brigade 45, 46-47, 53, 66
    19th Australian Brigade 53, 56, 57, 62
  armoured cars **20**, 56, **90**
  artillery 22, **52**, **60**, **62**, **69**, **77**
  attacks Italian supply columns 8-9
  Australian troops 22, 41, **44**, **45**, **60**, **78**, **87**, 88
    at Bardia **42-43**, **46**, 46-47, 48, 52-53
    at Beda Fomm 78, 84
    at Derna 65, 65-66, 66, 67-68, 68, 72, **72**
    at Tobruk **54**, 54, 56, 57, 61-62, 63, 64
  at Bardia **42-43**, 44-46, **46**, 46-47, 48, 49, 52-53, 54
  at Beda Fomm **70-71**, 73, 74-76, 76-77, 78-80, **79**(map), 80, 80-81, 84, 85
  captured equipment **34**, **54**, 62, **75**, **81**, 86
  casualties 11, 29, 36, 44, 52, 54, 64
  Combeforce 74-76, 76-77, 78, 79, 80, 84
  at Derna 65-66, 66, **66**(map), 67-68, 68, **72**, 72-73
  in Egypt 21
  at Enba Gap 29
  equipment 22
  the Five day raid 32, **32**, 32-33, 33, 34, 35-36, 37, 39, 40
  at Fort Capuzzo 8, **36**
  at Fort Maddalena 8
  Indian troops 22
  intelligence 27, 55
  Italian forces invade Egypt 11
  'Jock' Columns 12, 29
  logistics 29
  Mersa Matruh defence line, the **22**, **34**
  order of battle 25-26(table)
  quality of 93
  raids 8, 12
  reconnaissance 12, **60**
  reinforcements **23**, 27
  Royal Army Service Corps **58-59**
  security 37
  supplies 40, 55, 56, 69, 73
  tanks **2**, 22-23, **23**, **38**, **39**, **49**, 60, **60**, 61, 67, **68**, 69, 78, **80**
    at Tobruk 55, **55**(map), 56, 57, 61-63, 64
    delays 57, 60, 61
  training 22, 29, **40**
  transport 22, 45, **65**, 69
  Universal Carriers **36**
  victory party 86
  water 45
  weapons 22
    Boyes anti-tank rifle 8
    machine guns **48**
Buq Buq 37

casualties 11, 36, 87
  at Bardia 44, 52, 54
  at Enba Gap 29

at Tobruk 64
Caunter, Brigadier J. R. L. 8, 76, 79-80, 84
chronology 89
Churchill, Winston Leonard Spencer (1874-1965) 12-13, 15, 28, 29, 36-37, 54, 55
civilians **72**, **78**
Combe, Lieutenant-Colonel John 8, 9, 37, 74, 75, 76
Creagh, Major-General M. O'Moore 66, 67, 74, 78, 79
Cunningham, Admiral Sir Andrew Browne (1883-1963) **15**, 16

Dawes, Major A. **33**
Derna 65-69, 66(map), **72**, 72-73
dispositions **30-31**(map), **50-51**(map), **82-83**(map)
Dorman-Smith, Brigadier Eric 69, 72, 85

Eden, Anthony, British Secretary of State for War (1897-1977) 28, 54
Egypt 8, 21
  invasion of **10**(map)
Egyptian forces 21, **26**
El Adem 54
Enba Gap 29

Farouk, King of Egypt 21
Fort Capuzzo 8, **36**
Fort Maddalena 8
Fort Solaro 63
France 7
Free French forces 53

Gallina, Generale Sebastiano 35, 36
Gariboldi, Generale Italo 14
Godfrey, Lieutenant-Colonel 53-54
Gott, Brigadier William Henry Ewart (1897-1942) 11, 12
Graziani, Maresciallo Rodolfo (1882-1955) 11, 14, **14**, 38, 73
  plans 27
Great Britain 7
Greece 11, 12-13, 27, 27-28, 54, 55, 88

Halfaya Pass (Hellfire Pass) 11
Hitler, Adolf (1889-1945) 7
Hobart, Captain Pat 40
Hobart, Major-General Percy 22
Hughes, Trooper Eldred 77

Italian Air Force *see Regia Aeronautica*
Italian forces 7, **13**, 17
  Fifth Army 20
  Tenth Army 20, 65
    1st Libyan Division 35
  in Abyssinia 36
  artillery 20, **45**, **56**, **64**, **81**
  at Bardia 44, 47, **47**, 48, 49, 52, 53-54
  at Beda Fomm **70-71**, 76, 77, 78, 79-80, 80, 84, 85
  Bersaglieri 17, **18-19**
  casualties 11, 29, 64, 87
  deficiencies 21
  at Derna 65, 66, 68, 72-73
  dispositions 27
  at Enba Gap 29
  equipment 20
  Fascist Militia (*Milizia Volontaria par la Sicurrezza Nazionale* – MVSN) 17
  and the five Day raid 33, 34, 35, 36, 37, 39
  intelligence service 21, 27
  invasion of Egypt **10**(map), 11
  Libyan Tank Command 20
  losses 86-87
    at Maktila Camp 12
  native troops 17, 20
  order of battle 24(table)
  quality of troops 17, 33, 93
  reinforcements 11
  Royal Corps of Libyan Troops (*Regio Corpo di Truppe Libiche*) 17
  supply columns 8-9, 9
  tanks 8, **17**, 20, **47**, **74**, **76**
  at Tobruk 57, 63, 64
  transport 20-21, 27
  weapons 20, **75**

Italian Navy *see Regia Marina*

Jebel Akhdar, the 68

Ladybird, HMS 13, 32, 40, 46
Libya **21**
Lomax, Brigadier C. E. N. 35
Longmore, Air Chief Marshal Sir Arthur 13, **15**, 15-16, 55
looting **93**

Mackay, Major-General Iven 44, 46, 52, 60-61, 64, 68
Maktila 12, 32, 35
Maletti, Generale Pietro 33
Malta 7-8, **9**, **12**
Manella, Generale Petassi 57, 63
Mechili 66, **66**(map)
Mediterranean theatre, the **6**(map), 7
Mersa Matruh defence line, the **22**, **34**
Mussolini, Benito (1883-1945) 7, **7**, 11, 14

Nezuet Ghirba 9
Nibeiwa Camp, attack on 32-33

O'Connor, Lieutenant-General Richard Nugent (1889-1981) 15, **16**, 35, 36, 38, 56, 87
  at Bardia 44, 46, 52
  at Beda Fomm 84
  at Derna 66, 66-67, 68-69
  plans 28-29, 44, 69, 73
  success 85
  at Tobruk 55, 57, 60

Petherick, Lieutenant-Colonel W. G. **33**
Pickett, Corporal A. A. 48
prisoners 33, 34, 36, 37, 44, 47, 48, 49, 53, **53**, 63, 64, 77, 84, 86, **86**, **94**

Regia Aeronautica (Italian Air Force) 7, 11, 13, 21, 37, 39, **67**, **73**, 87
  order of battle 24(table)
Regia Marina (Italian Navy) 7, 21
Royal Air Force 11, 13, 23, 27, 32, 37, 54, 61
  ascendancy of 16, 36
  losses 87
  order of battle 26(table)
Royal Australian Air Force 54, **64**
Royal Navy 7, 9, 11, 13, 23, 38, 46, 49, 61
  Fleet Air Arm **8**, **12**

San Giorgio **61**, 64
Sidi Barrani 11, **28**, 32
Sidi Omar 39-40
Sidi Saleh 75, 79
Siret el Chreiba 65-66
Sollum 38, **44**, 45
Somerville, Captain Tom **33**
Suez Canal, the 21

Taranto, raid on **8**, 21
Tellera, Generale Giuseppe **15**
Terror, HMS 32, 40, 46, 61
Tobruk 9, 14, 54-57, **55**(map), **57**, 60-64, 69
Tripoli 87, 88
Tummar East, attack on 34
Tummar West, attack on 33-34

Valiant, HMS 49

Wadi el Kharruba 35
wargaming 93-95
Warspite, HMS **35**, 49
Wavell, General Sir Archibald Percival (1883-1950) **15**, 54, 55
  background 14-15
  and O'Connor's plans 69, 72
  and Operation Compass 29, 87
  plans 27, 28, 87-88
  security 37
  simplifies chain of command 56
Wilson, Lieutenant-General Sir Henry Maitland (1881-1964) 15, **16**, 56